OUR HOLY FAITH
A RELIGION SERIES for THE ELEMENTARY SCHOOLS

TEACHER'S MANUAL for

Jesus Comes

**Based on the First Communion Catechism
Confraternity Edition**

Sister Mary Naomi, O.S.U., M.A.
Sister Mary Florentine, H.H.M., B.S.E.
with the assistance of
Sister Mary Clarice, O.S.U., M.A.
Sister Mary Daniel, O.S.U., B.S.E.
and others

ST. AUGUSTINE ACADEMY PRESS
HOMER GLEN, ILLINOIS

Nihil obstat:

JOHN F. MURPHY, S.T.D.
Censor librorum

Imprimatur:

✠ WILLIAM E. COUSINS
Archbishop of Milwaukee

March 1, 1960

This book was originally published in 1960
by Bruce Publishing, Milwaukee.

This reprinted edition ©2017 by St. Augustine Academy Press
ISBN: 978-1-64051-016-6

CONTENTS

IN HUMBLE GRATITUDE
THIS WORK IS DEDICATED TO
ST. PIUS X
THE POPE OF THE HOLY EUCHARIST

GENERAL INTRODUCTION FOR THE SERIES

OUR HOLY FAITH

The Series, OUR HOLY FAITH, is intended to provide a complete, integrated, and basic course in religion for the eight grades of the elementary school.

The purpose of teaching religion in the elementary school is to see to it that the pupil has a clear and adequate knowledge of his holy Faith, so as to guide and influence his will to use grace in forming the image of Christ in himself. While primarily addressed to the intellect, it does not neglect the will or the child's attitudes and emotions. The first purpose of this religion Series, therefore, is clear and adequate knowledge of the Catholic religion.

The psychological basis for this is to be found in St. Augustine's little gem, "On Catechizing the Unlettered."*

St. Augustine tells us that in teaching religion we must lead the pupil from faith, to hope, to charity. The first step, therefore, is knowledge of our religion based on supernatural faith. The child is taught and accepts what Christ's Church, through her representative, proposes to be believed.

Content and Arrangement of the Series — Grades 1 and 2

The content of the first two grades is the traditional content of those grades, with emphasis on Confession and Holy Communion in the second grade.

Grades 3, 4, and 5

The first two grades are followed by two cycles of three grades each — 3 to 5 and 6 to 8. In Grades 3, 4, and 5, the No. 1 Baltimore Catechism is followed in the exact sequence of its lessons and indeed of its questions, in such fashion, however, that the first half of the No. 1 Revised Baltimore Catechism** (the Creed and the first three Commandments) is covered in the first book of that sequence (GOD'S TRUTHS HELP US LIVE); the second half of the No. 1 Catechism is covered in the third book of that sequence (OUR FAITH: GOD'S GREAT GIFT). The second book of that sequence (THE VINE AND THE BRANCHES) is devoted to a study of the liturgy and the liturgical year. In this book the catechetical approach is, for obvious reasons, omitted. We have placed this material, which deals with an important area of religious instruction omitted in the Catechism, between two books devoted to explaining the Catechism.

Thus, the suggested sequence for Grades 3 to 5 is:

Grade 3 — GOD'S TRUTHS HELP US LIVE
(First half of No. 1 Catechism)

Grade 4 — THE VINE AND THE BRANCHES
(The liturgy and the liturgical year)

Grade 5 — LIVING LIKE CHRIST IN CHRIST
(Second half of No. 1 Catechism)

One value of this sequence is that it provides an alternation from the Catechism, applying the same doctrines but in a completely different manner.

Grades 6, 7, and 8

The books for the three remaining grades — 6, 7, and 8 — are similarly organized. In the first book of the sequence, OUR FAITH: GOD'S GREAT GIFT, the pupil studies the first half of the No. 2 Revised Baltimore Catechism. The second half of the No. 2 Catechism is then taken up in the volume, TO LIVE IS CHRIST, which is recommended for Grade 8 because it contains a review of the first half of the No. 2 Catechism and an intense study of its second half. The third book in this sequence (recommended for Grade 7, but usable in any grade from the sixth to the eighth) is entitled CHRIST: IN PROPHECY, IN PERSON, AND IN HIS CHURCH. It contains a complete chronological treatment of Bible History and of Church History, which have often been neglected in recent courses of study. The suggested sequence for Grades 6 to 8 is this:

Grade 6 — OUR FAITH: GOD'S GREAT GIFT
(First half of No. 2 Catechism)

Grade 7 — CHRIST: IN PROPHECY, IN PERSON, AND IN HIS CHURCH
(Bible History — Church History)

Grade 8 — TO LIVE IS CHRIST
(Second half of No. 2 Catechism)

Flexibility of the Series

Although the Series follows the sequence of the Catechism, its subject matter is so arranged that it is pos-

---

* There are many translations; that of Rev. Joseph P. Christopher, *De catechizandis Rudibus* (Washington, D. C.: Catholic University, 1926), is very good.

** All references to the Catechism are to the Confraternity Edition.

sible for a superintendent, a pastor, or a principal to adapt it to almost every course of study for religion in the elementary grades, or vice versa, to adapt the course of study to fit the Series. Since it contains books that are devoted to a study of the liturgy and of biblical and Church history, the Series makes it possible for the teacher to break up the monotony that frequently results from studying nothing but the Catechism year after year.

It is suggested that the book covering the first half of the No. 1 Catechism be used in Grade 3 and that the one dealing with the second half be employed for Grade 5, with the book on the liturgy for Grade 4. However the order of sequence can be changed if another order seems more appropriate. The book on the liturgy, THE VINE AND THE BRANCHES, can be postponed to Grade 5 if it is thought too difficult for Grade 4 (it is, however, no more difficult than science or geography in that grade); or it can be anticipated in an earlier grade or even completely omitted. The latter possibility, however, is one which the authors hope is not considered. Our present courses of study in elementary religion almost universally omit an ordered and intensive study of the liturgy and the liturgical year, which, as Pope Pius XII reminded us, is a basic means of religious instruction.

Method of Handling the Catechism

In the past, the method of teaching religion in the elementary schools was, quite justly, criticized for its misuse of the Catechism. The fault certainly did not lie in the Catechism, which is intended as a concise and precise synopsis of religious knowledge. The Catechism is designed to be studied carefully *after* it has been taught and explained authoritatively in the name of the Church.

Too often, however, the authoritative teaching and presentation has been omitted, and the child has been led directly to the bald, synoptic questions and answers of the Catechism, which he has been directed to study before or without any explanation and then repeat in rote fashion after he has memorized them.

Fortunately, in most modern courses of study in religion this abuse has been eliminated. The result has been courses of study more enjoyable to teacher and pupil alike.

Unfortunately, in many instances, the Catechism has also been abandoned. Bishops and pastors have deplored this, with great justification. An ordered knowledge of one's religion is absolutely necessary, and this the Catechism insures.

In this Series we have retained the exact sequence of the Catechisms No. 1 and No. 2. However, we have taken care to teach the content of the lessons *before* asking the child to study and, if needed, to memorize the Catechism questions and answers. Thus we hope we have met the reasonable desires of the clergy, by accenting the Catechism, while not forgetting the needs and problems of the pupils and teachers in the classroom.

In many instances, while following the Catechism, we have added points not covered in it but necessary either as matters of knowledge or as material aiding assimilation and application of the basic doctrines. Our intention has been to make the study of religion as attractive and enjoyable and as instructive as possible. In short, we believe that a child's attitude toward religion is as important as his knowledge. One without the other is not of much value, and in this Series we have sought to integrate the two.

In this connection, however, let it be clearly stated and understood that the child's inclination or enjoyment is not the prime factor to be considered. We are dealing here with a matter that is not subject to the likes or dislikes of the pupil. Here we are concerned with a divinely constituted body of knowledge which the Church has a mandate to convey to the human race, and particularly to her members, in an authoritative way. "As the Father hath sent me, I also send you. Going therefore . . ." (Mt. 28:28).

Here, a curriculum determined by child interest or enjoyment would be an absurdity.

A Key Point— The Answer Before the Question

In the four years in which the texts of the Series are based directly on the Catechism — Grades 3, 5, 6, and 8 — we have included the Catechism answers in the body of the lessons, using the exact words of the Catechism; but, we have expanded, paraphrased, and otherwise explained the meaning of the Catechism; this will insure that the child understands what the Catechism means, and will assist him to learn it when he studies the Catechism questions and answers at the end of the lesson. *The Catechism answers have been placed in boldface or in italics* to call attention to them. Thus, we teach the answer before we ask the child to learn it. The result is *understanding*, not mere rote memorization.

BASIC PRINCIPLES IN TEACHING RELIGION

What follows are the essential and fundamental principles for the teaching of religion. All else is accidental.

Begin With Faith

The first objective of the teaching of religion is a knowledge of the truths God wants us to know, and an acceptance of those truths on the basis of God's veracity — namely, an informed but unhesitating faith.

End With Love

The supreme objective of the teaching of religion, however, is not faith but love — love of God. The objective we have had in building this Series, and the objective the teachers of religion must have in teaching it, is to lead the pupil to a supernatural love of God.

With St. Augustine we ask every teacher of this Series to refer everything she teaches to the love of God — God's love for us as proved by what He has done for us, and our love of God as proved by how we serve God in Himself and in our neighbors.

With God's love for us and ours for Him ever in mind, the teacher should present the doctrines and moral precepts of the Catholic religion in such a fashion that they lead the child first to an appreciation of his faith and a strengthening of that virtue in him; then to an increase of hope in him, for without supernatural hope there will be no continued striving.

The end, however, is love. The pupil should be led to see in everything that God has done an evidence of His love for us. He has loved us enough to reveal to us what He wants us to believe. He has revealed His existence, the incarnation, the redemption, the Church, the sacraments, the moral code we follow, the rewards He has in store for us, and so many other matters. In each of these truths He is proving His love for us. They should be so taught that, in all, God's love of us may stand out and arouse a desire to return love for love.

If truths are so taught, it will be easy for the child to see his obligation to love and serve God in return. They will not then be merely abstract truths with little personal meaning, but will become knowledge charged with motives for the will to requite that divine love.

Method and Content Intertwined

From the above it will be seen that method and content in the proper teaching of religion are closely intertwined. The point to be learned is first presented to the intellect as an object of faith and knowledge, then related to hope, as being possible, and finally to love as being something to be desired and possessed. All other details of methodology should be subordinated to this basic sequence.

It is all the more necessary to insist on this because the unit method we have used is also commonly employed in teaching the social studies. There, however, it is not based on supernatural virtues, but on the natural intellectual virtues.

Christian Formation

The formation of the perfect Christian, whose life is patterned on the life of Christ, is our final goal. This cannot be achieved by teaching or by the school. It is a supernatural task, requiring supernatural means. These means are in the possession of the Church. All the teacher can do is instruct and influence the pupil to fulfill his destiny as a member of Christ's Mystical Body, to see his role in the sacrifice it offers to the heavenly Father, to utilize the channels of grace it offers him. Solid, accurate, and full instruction by the teacher means much, but it does not guarantee the co-operation of the student. He still has his free will. The teacher can instruct, give good example, and pray — in doing these she does much. The home, too, can do much. But the grace of God, the Church and her means of grace, and the free will of the individual are all-important. We must do our utmost to enlighten the intellect and train the will of our charges — then leave the rest to God.

II. INTRODUCTION FOR THIS GRADE

Theme: God Watches Over Us.

The unifying theme for the second grade course of study is the providence of God, the theme that *God Watches Over Us.*

The basic truths of religion taught in the second grade are: the Commandments and the Sacraments of Penance and Holy Eucharist. These are developed in Units 3, 4, and 5. The other units cover such topics as:

1. the basic truths about God that are found in the Apostles' Creed;
2. the angels;
3. the Sacrament of Baptism;
4. incidents in the lives of Christ, our Blessed Mother, the saints, and some Old Testament figures;
5. material on the three principal parts of the Mass.

The virtues and activities suggested are meant to apply and carry over into the child's daily life the doctrine taught in the religion lessons. They should help the child see how he can model his life on that of the Child Jesus.

The pupil text, *Jesus Comes*, is merely a *supplement* to this teachers' manual. This means that it should be used only after a development lesson found in the manual or a series of such lessons have been covered. Then only should the teacher ask the pupils to read in the text, the material already treated in class. The children should then be ready for a *discussion.* After this a *drill lesson*, based on the questions at the end of each lesson or lessons, should be given. These questions are indicated in the manual under pupil text (*Jesus Comes*) at the end of each lesson.

Thus the teaching steps involved in the second grade course of study are:

1. Development lesson(s)
2. Reading of the text by pupils
3. Discussion
4. Drill lesson on catechism questions

A lesson plan illustrating each type of the above lessons will be found in this *Teacher's Manual* and *Course of Study*, hereafter, referred to as *Manual.*

The material of the first four units have been organized, within the units, into weekly blocks. The first four days of the week are devoted to the teaching and studying of the material; the fifth day to a review, further drill if necessary, and an application to the children's lives of the truths learned during the week.

This allocation of the material into weekly blocks is not to be followed slavishly. The teacher must judge when to break away from it, finishing the material in fewer days or taking more than five days if that seems best for the pupils.

The material of each unit is summarized by a general review at the end.

N.B. The references in each unit will furnish adequate material for both teacher and pupil. The bold face numbers refer to the keyed references in the teacher's bibliography at the end of this *Manual*, pp. 92–93.

II. UNITS OF STUDY AND APPROXIMATE TIME ALLOTMENTS

General Theme: God Watches Over Us

Unit One — How Our Heavenly Father Takes Care of Us — 7 weeks

Unit Two — How Some People Obeyed God — 7 weeks

Unit Three — How We Should Obey God — 7 weeks

Unit Four — How God Pardons Us When We Sin — 6 weeks

Unit Five — How God Cares for Our Souls Through the Holy Eucharist — 7 weeks

Unit Six — How We can Show Our Love for God: The Practice of Religion — 3 weeks

GENERAL OBJECTIVES

A. Knowledge

1. To learn that God watches over each one of us with loving care.
2. To learn how God showed His infinite goodness in the work of creation.
3. To learn of God's love for creatures and the return which they made.
4. To understand the necessity of working with creatures to carry out God's plan.
5. To learn about the attributes of God shown to us through the work of creation.
6. To realize that prayer is one means of showing gratitude to God.
7. To learn to say the assigned prayers correctly and devoutly.
8. To learn to make simple meditations.
9. To learn that our main purpose in life is to do God's will.
10. To develop a meaningful vocabulary of words and phrases used in religion.
11. To learn how the commandments are an expression of God's will.
12. To understand that God gave us certain laws to help us save our souls.
13. To learn the necessity of grace, which comes through the reception of the Sacraments of Baptism, Penance, and Holy Eucharist.

B. Virtue

1. To grow in love of God because of His loving care.
2. To practice the virtues of faith, hope, and love.
3. To form the habit of using created things to make us more Christlike.
4. To bring others to Christ by our Christlike living.
5. To learn the practice of self-control in the use of created things.
6. To co-operate with God's grace in developing habits of virtue and avoiding sin in our daily life.
7. To cultivate a sense of sorrow for our ingratitude toward God.
8. To develop an attitude of love and submission to God's laws.

9. To love and respect all men because they are children of God.
10. To cultivate love and devotion to God, the angels, and the saints.
11. To find in the lives of the Holy Family and the saints perfect examples of obedience.
12. To imitate the examples of obedience given us by the Holy Family and the saints.
13. To learn to love vocal and mental prayer.
14. To love and appreciate the use of the Sacraments of Penance and Holy Eucharist.

A SUGGESTED DEVELOPMENT LESSON PLAN

I. SUBJECT MATTER

God's First Creatures: The Angels (Cf. p. 12, Third Day)

II. TYPE

Development

III. OBJECTIVES

A. To acquaint the children with the creation of the angels.
B. To develop the realization that angels are pure spirits.
C. To instill the knowledge that the angels were created to adore and glorify God, to do His will, and to show His goodness.

IV. SUGGESTED PROCEDURE

A. Approach

Do you remember when I told you that in the beginning there was only God? He alone existed; there was nothing else. Would you like to hear today about the first creatures God created or made and why He created them? What creature do you think God created first? Discuss.

B. Presentation

1. The Angels

Before the world was created, no one can tell how long ago, God created or made His first creatures. He did so out of goodness, for He was perfectly happy and wanted to make others so that they could share His happiness. Thus He created the angels. When God created the angels, He made them very beautiful. The most beautiful thing here on earth cannot be as beautiful as an angel. Artists have tried to paint angels. They have given them beautiful faces, rich and lovely garments, and graceful wings; but, really angels are so beautiful that no artist can paint them as beautiful as they really are. God created a great number of angels. God made them just to show His love and goodness and to share with them His happiness and life.

2. Nature of the Angels

Angels are pure spirits; that means that they have no bodies. God made them. Artists paint them with bodies to try to show us how very beautiful angels are; but really they have no bodies, for they are pure spirits. We cannot see them.

God made the angels wise, powerful, and holy. They do not have to study as we do; they know everything at once. They are not as powerful as God; yet they have great power, power next to God's. That is why we should often pray to the angels for help.

3. Why God Created the Angels

Why do you think God created the angels? He created them to show His goodness, to make them happy. He made them to adore, love, and do God's will in heaven and on earth.

Some people tell us there are no angels, because they cannot be seen. We cannot see the electricity that makes our lights glow, can we? We do not say there is no such thing as electricity just because we cannot see it, do we? (Discuss)

I wonder what our book has to say about the angels. Let us open our text to Lesson Three, page 20. Now look at question (17). (Give the class enough time to read the question and answer.) Can anyone tell me now why God created or made the angels? Yes, to love and adore Him. If we love someone we will do what that person asks us to do. We will be happy to do it, won't we? That is doing His will. That is what God wanted and expected the angels to do also. Sometimes God wants His angels to bring messages to men, as the Angel Gabriel, who carried God's message to the Blessed Virgin Mary. Sometimes He sent them to protect people, or to protect a certain city or village. Some angels were created just to love and adore God in heaven. Don't you think God is wonderful to create the angels? He creates them just to make them happy by sharing heaven with them, and to show His goodness. Tomorrow I will tell you more about God's angels.

C. Organization

1. Who were the first creatures God created?
2. What is an angel?
3. How many angels did God create?
4. Do angels have bodies like ours? Why not?
5. Why do artists draw pictures of them with bodies and wings?
6. What were the wonderful gifts God gave the angels?
7. Why did God create the angels?
8. What do we mean when we say the angels "do God's will"?

D. Virtues and Practices

1. Offer our work and play today for God's glory.
2. Often think of our angel at our side.

E. Assignment

Catechism Questions 16, 17 at the end of Lesson 3 in text.

V. SUGGESTED LEARNING ACTIVITIES

A. Discuss pictures of angels to find out why they are pictured with bodies and wings.
B. Discuss angels doing different things for God.
C. Read and discuss the poem "The Angels." (Cf. "The Angels" from the book *Sing a Song of Holy Things* by Sister M. Josita, O.S.F. Published by the Tower Press, Milwaukee, 1945.)

VI. REFERENCES AND MATERIALS

A. Teacher's References
   1. Morrow, Louis, *My Catholic Faith*, My Mission House, Kenosha, Wis.
   2. Josita Belger, Sister, *Sing a Song of Holy Things*, Tower Press, Milwaukee, Wis.
   3. Schumacher, Vol. I, *I Teach Catechism*, Benziger Brothers, Inc., Chicago, Ill.
B. Pupil Text
   Jesus Comes, Bruce, Milwaukee.

(*Additional models of Development Lessons will be found at the head of Units Two to Six.*)

A SUGGESTED DISCUSSION LESSON PLAN

I. SUBJECT MATTER

How the Good Angels Help Us by Serving as Our Guardians (Cf. p. 14, Second Day)

II. TYPE

Discussion

III. OBJECTIVES

A. To help each pupil realize that he has a powerful helper in his guardian angel.
B. To teach the children to have a daily devotion to their own guardian angel and to all the angels.

IV. SUGGESTED PROCEDURE

A. Approach

Do we know why God gave each of us a guardian angel?

B. Presentation

1. Set up standards for the discussion.
   a) Help the children to formulate a few rules to be followed in a discussion lesson, e.g.:
      1) Everyone takes part.
      2) Speak clearly.
      3) Keep to the subject.
      4) Help others to take part.
      5) Be polite.
      6) Be a good listener.
      7) Ask questions.
   b) The teacher should write two or three of these rules on the blackboard as they are suggested by the children.
2. Present the material to be discussed.
   a) The teacher may adapt and tell the story: "Tobias' Journey" — *Bible Lessons*, Horan, p. 115.
   b) Bring out the fact that God sent the angel to guard Tobias on this journey. He also has

sent an angel to each human person to guide and direct his way through life.

   c) Emphasize Tobias' obedience to the angel.

   d) Stress the importance of the children's devotion to their guardian angels.

   e) Point out the importance of prayer to our guardian angel in times of temptation and danger.

C. Generalization

Have the pupils give in sentences some important points they wish to remember as a result of the discussion.

D. Virtues to Practice

Have the children form resolutions resulting from this discussion, such as:

1. Ask their guardian angels to keep them safe in times of danger and temptation.
2. Pray daily to their guardian angels.
3. Thank God for His goodness in giving them each a guardian angel.

E. Organization

1. Why did young Tobias go on this trip?
2. What kind of man did Tobias wish for to take his son on this journey?
3. When Tobias was washing his feet in the river he became very frightened. Why?
4. What did the young man tell Tobias to do with the fish?
5. Was the fish of any use to them after it was killed?
6. How was Tobias' father cured of his blindness?
7. How did old Tobias want to reward the young man?
8. When did Tobias find out that the young man was really an angel?
9. How did the young man let Tobias know he was an angel?
10. How do you think this story proves that angels protect people?
11. When should we especially ask our guardian angels for help?
12. Do you know a prayer to your guardian angel?

F. Assignment

Catechism question 22, Lesson 3, pupil text.

V. SUGGESTED LEARNING ACTIVITIES

A. Dramatize the story, or the part they like best.
B. Tell the story of Tobias and the angel to younger brothers and sisters at home.
C. Draw pictures of ways in which their guardian angels help them.

VI. REFERENCE AND MATERIAL

A. Story: Tobias' Journey, *Bible Lessons*, p. 115.
B. Pupil text: *Jesus Comes.*

A SUGGESTED DRILL LESSON PLAN

I. SUBJECT MATTER

Our Heavenly Father Takes Care of Us

II. TYPE

Drill (To be used after Lessons 1, 2, and 3 in *Jesus Comes*)

III. OBJECTIVES

A. To check orally on the material covered in catechism Lessons 1, 2, and 3.
B. To help children to make use of this knowledge in their daily life.

IV. PROCEDURE

A. Approach

Today we are going to see how well we know what we have learned in the first three lessons of our catechism. How many think they will know all the answers?

B. Presentation

1. The pupils answer orally all the questions stressed in Lessons 1, 2, and 3 of pupil text. (A drill lesson does not take the form of a discussion lesson. It should be a rapid question and answer period.)

C. Activities: Games

1. *Divided Statements:* This activity may best be used with catechism answers. One child on Team A gives the first part of a catechism answer, such as, "Angels are spirits. . . ." He calls on a member of Team B to give the remainder of the sentence: ". . . created by God." Team A may have ten turns and then reverse.

2. *King of the Mountain:* The teacher draws a crown at the top of the blackboard with stairs leading up on each side. If a correct response is given to a "yes-no" question, or to a catechism question, the child or captain writes "B" or "G" (if the game is boys vs. girls) or "A" or "B" (if the teams are mixed) on the first step. The opposing team then responds and places the corresponding mark on its step if the answer is correct. The team reaching the crown first is "King of the Mountain."

3. *Double or Nothing:* This is simply a different device for keeping score of points earned in a catechism quiz. The first correct answer merits one point, the second 2, the third 4, the fourth 8, the fifth 16, the sixth 32, etc. For a variation: if one team reaches 64 too fast, make the team start over with one point each time someone misses.

D. Application

Do you think you have learned these catechism questions? Which do you think is more important, knowing all these questions and answers just to show we are smart or knowing them because they help us to know, love, and serve God better? We should then make up our minds to love God who showed His love for us by creating everything in this world and then by giving us the angels to help us get to heaven and to Him.

UNIT I. *HOW OUR HEAVENLY FATHER TAKES CARE OF US*

I. INTRODUCTION FOR THE TEACHER

This unit presents for study the basic truths about God that are found in the Apostles' Creed. The prayers, practices of virtue, and suggested activities listed for each day help lead the child to a better understanding and a deeper appreciation of his duty to God.

II. OBJECTIVES

A. To learn how the angels do God's will.
B. To cultivate love and devotion for the angels.
C. To learn that God showed His love for us through the work of creation.
D. To learn the attributes of God as shown in creation.
E. To understand and appreciate God's plan in creating man.
F. To learn of God's mercy in spite of man's ingratitude.
G. To have a clear understanding of God's goodness, mercy, and justice.
H. To cultivate a deep feeling of gratitude to God for the gifts He has given us.
I. To practice the virtues of faith, hope, and love in our daily lives.
J. To make simple meditations.

III. SUBJECT MATTER

A. The creation of the angels.
B. How almighty God created the world for us and keeps it in order. — How these creatures do God's will.
C. God's great love and goodness in creating and saving us.
D. What we can do for God through prayer.

THINGS TO KNOW

	CONTENT	PUPIL TEXT	CHURCH YEAR	PRAYERS AND HYMNS
1st DAY	A. The Creation of the Angels. 1. God's Loving Care: Divine Providence: God creates the things we need. God watches over us and keeps us from harm. God helps us with His sacraments.		September 8 Nativity of the Blessed Virgin	Review Our Father Pupil Text — page 1
2nd DAY	God, the Creator of all things: 1. There is one God. 2. There are Three Persons in one God.	Lessons I, II Questions 1–5 Page 15 Questions 6–14 Page 17		Review Sign of the Cross Pupil Text — page 1 Review Glory be to the Father Pupil Text — page 2

3rd DAY	2. God's First Creatures: The Angels:
	
	a) nature of the angels: pure spirits
	b) why God created them:
	  1) to give Him honor and glory
	  2) to do His will in heaven and on earth
		Lesson 3
		Questions 15–17
		Page 20
				Review
				
				Angel of God, My Guardian Dear
				Pupil Text — page 4

4th DAY	3. How the good angels help us as messengers: a) the Archangel Gabriel			Review Hail Mary Pupil Text — page 2
5th DAY	Brief review, drill, and application to life of the basic truths learned during this week.			

THINGS TO DO

VIRTUES AND PRACTICES	SUGGESTED LEARNING ACTIVITIES	REFERENCES AND MATERIALS
1. Watch for things God does to take care of you during the day: a) your Catholic homes b) your Catholic schools 2. Thank God for these blessings.	1. Show pictures of way in which God takes care of us. 2. Draw pictures of the ways in which God takes care of us today. 3. Practice behavior and reverence in church. 4. Tell the story of the Nativity of the B.V.M., No. **16**, p. 13. (See note below.)*	Baierl, *The Creed Explained*, p. 132 (cf. No. **11**, p. 92).*
1. Make the Sign of the Cross devoutly to honor the Blessed Trinity.	1. Use symbols for the Trinity and Unity of God, No. **24**, p. 396.* Use record: The Sign of the Cross from the Catholic Children's Record Album. 2. Read and discuss the poem, "Blessed Trinity," No. **57**, p. 6.* 3. Suggested filmstrip: God and His Perfections, The St. John's Catechism Filmstrip Series (cf. No. **67**, Units 1, 2).*	Baierl, *The Creed Explained*, p. 132 (cf. No. **11**, p. 92).* Morrow, *My Catholic Faith* (cf. No. **24**, p. 92).*
1. Offer your work and play today for God's glory.	1. Discuss pictures of angels to find out why they are shown with bodies and wings. 2. Discuss pictures of angels doing different things for God (cf. No. **62**, p. 114).* 3. Read and discuss the poem: "The Angels," No. **57**, p. 10.* 4. Sing a hymn to the guardian angel. 5. Suggested filmstrip: Creation of the Angels (cf. No. **67**, Unit 3).*	Baierl, *The Creed Explained*, p. 149 (cf. No. **11**, p. 92).* Morrow, *My Catholic Faith* (cf. No. **24**, p. 92).*
1. Do little duties faithfully today because that is what God wants you to do.	1. Dramatize the story of the "Annunciation." 2. Read and discuss the poem "Annunciation," No. **57**, p. 17.* 3. Read and discuss the poem "Hail, Full of Grace," No. **57**, p. 55.*	Morrow, *My Catholic Faith*, pp. 30–31 (cf. No. **24**, p. 92).*

* For all keyed references in boldface type, see Teacher Bibliography, pp. 92–93, at end of this Teacher's Manual.

THINGS TO KNOW

	CONTENT	PUPIL TEXT	CHURCH YEAR	PRAYERS AND HYMNS
1st DAY	*b)* Angels at the Nativity *c)* Angels in the Flight into Egypt		September 12 The Most Holy Name of the Blessed Virgin	"Glory to God in the highest, peace on earth to men of good will."
2nd DAY	4. How the good angels help us as our guardians: *a)* the Archangel Raphael *b)* St. Cecilia and her guardian angel *c)* the duties of guardian angels *d)* devotions to the guardian angels and to all the angels	Lesson 3 Question 22 Page 21		"St. Raphael, the Archangel, pray for us." "Angel of God, My Guardian Dear." Pupil Text — page 4
3rd DAY	5. How God tested the angels: *a)* God's justice in rewarding the good angels *b)* God's justice in punishing the bad angels	Lesson 3 Questions 19–20 Page 21	September 15 The Seven Sorrows of the Blessed Virgin	Have the pupils memorize the Act of Contrition. See: Pupil Text — page 5
4th DAY	6. How the bad angels harm us by trying to make us do wrong.	Lesson 3 Question 23 Page 21		Original prayers to our guardian angel.
5th DAY	Brief review, drill, and application to life of the basic truths learned during this 2nd week.			

14

THINGS TO DO

VIRTUES AND PRACTICES	SUGGESTED LEARNING ACTIVITIES	REFERENCES AND MATERIALS
1. Make others happy by being courteous.	1. Children tell what they would have done if they had been the angels at the Nativity, No. **16**, p. 21.* 2. Dramatize the story of "Flight into Egypt," No. **16**, p. 39.* 3. Read and discuss the poem, "The Flight into Egypt" (cf. No. **60**, p. 25).*	Moran, *Verses for Tiny Tots*, p. 24 (cf. No. **60**, p. 93).*
1. Pray to your guardian angel in time of temptation. 2. Ask the help and seek the advice of your guardian angel.	1. Attentive listening to story of "Archangel Raphael" in preparation for class discussion, No. **3**, p. 115.* 2. Children dramatize the parts of the story they like best. 3. Show picture of St. Cecilia: Read and discuss the poem "St. Cecilia," No. **57**, p. 22.* 4. Illustrate the times when my angel helps me, No. **38**, pp. 32–36.*	Horan, *Bible Lessons* (cf. No. **3**, p. 92).*
1. Watch for times when God tests your obedience.	1. Attentive listening to the story of "Michael the Archangel" in preparation for class discussion, No. **32**, Vol. I.*	Baierl, *The Creed Explained*, p. 154 (cf. No. **11**, p. 92).*
1. Say "No" to temptation because your guardian angel is with you.	1. Discuss the various ways in which the bad angels make wrong look "good."	Morrow, *My Catholic Faith*, pp. 32–33 (cf. No. **24**, p. 92).*

* For all keyed references in boldface type, see Teacher Bibliography, pp. 92–93, at end of this Teacher's Manual.

THINGS TO KNOW

	CONTENT	PUPIL TEXT	CHURCH YEAR	PRAYERS AND HYMNS
1st DAY	B. How almighty God created the world for you and keeps it in existence: How creatures carry out God's will: 1. The creation of light and sky: sun, moon, and stars.	Lesson 4 Question 24 Page 26		"My God, I believe You can do all things." Say prayers to thank God for His loving care in sending us all kinds of weather.
2nd DAY	2. The creation of land, water, and plants.			Review Grace before and after meals. See: Pupil Text — Page 7
3rd DAY	3. The creation of animals: fish, birds, and land animals.			Original prayers of thanksgiving for the gift of creation.
4th DAY	4. How these creatures help us know God's beauty and power.		September 21 St. Matthew	Mental Prayer: 1. Think of God's beauty and power. 2. Tell Him how beautiful He is. 3. Ask Him to help us.
5th DAY	Brief review, drill, and application to life of the basic truths learned during this 3rd week.			

THINGS TO DO

VIRTUES AND PRACTICES	SUGGESTED LEARNING ACTIVITIES	REFERENCES AND MATERIALS
The Practice of Hope 1. Take the kind of weather God sends you cheerfully because He knows what is best.	1. Begin a frieze on Creation.	Baierl, *The Creed Explained*, p. 132 (cf. No. **11**, p. 92).
1. When your parents give you food to eat, thank them and God, who is the source of all the goods you receive.	1. Continue work on the frieze of Creation. 2. Read the poems: No. **61**, pp. 32, 56, 57: "Daisies" "Forget-me-nots" "My Land is God's Land" 3. Follow with a class discussion of each.	Johnson, *The Bible Story*, p. 3 (cf. No. **4**, p. 92). Horan, *Bible Lessons*, p. 1 (cf. No. **3**, p. 92).
1. Be kind to animals because God has created them.	1. Continue work on the frieze of Creation. 2. Learn "All Things Bright and Beautiful."	Same reference as above.
1. Thank God for His gifts by taking good care of them. 2. Ask God to help you with your work during the day because He can do all things.	1. Collect pictures to illustrate God's Beauty and Power. 2. Read and discuss poem "God's Help" and "The Wonderful World," No. **58**, p. 26.	Dennerle, *Leading the Little Ones to Christ*, p. 25 (cf. No. **14**, p. 92).

THINGS TO KNOW

	CONTENT	PUPIL TEXT	CHURCH YEAR	PRAYERS AND HYMNS
1st DAY	C. God's great love and goodness in creating and saving us. 1. The creation of the first man and woman: *a*) man made to the image and likeness of God: body and soul	Lesson 4 Question 25 Page 26		"Dear God, each day make me more like You."

2nd DAY	*b*) the happiness of Adam and Eve in Paradise.
	
	  1) gifts given to Adam:
	    (*a*) sanctifying grace
	    (*b*) a perfect body
	    (*c*) freedom from sickness
	    (*d*) immortality
	    (*e*) freedom from work
	    (*f*) knowledge
		Lesson 4
		Questions 26–27
		Page 26
				Selections from the Breastplate of St. Patrick.

3rd DAY	2. How Adam and Eve disobeyed God — story of the temptation and fall:
	
	  a) how Adam and Eve knew their sin: the voice of conscience
	  b) how God knew their sin: God is everywhere, knows all, and sees all
		Lesson 4
		Questions 28–29
		Page 26
		
		Lesson 2
		Questions 6, 7
		Page 17
				Short prayers such as "All for Jesus."

4th DAY	*c*) How God showed His Justice and Mercy:
	
	  1) the punishments of God: how they affect us
	  2) the nature of original sin
	  3) the promise of the Saviour
	  4) why Mary was free from original sin
	  5) God becomes man to save us from sin.
		Lesson 4
		Questions 31, 32, 33, 34, 35–36
		Pages 26–27
				Review
				
				Act of Consecration
				
				Mental Prayer:
				
				Think of Mary and her beautiful soul.

5th DAY	Brief review, drill, and application to life of the basic truths learned during this 4th week.			

THINGS TO DO

VIRTUES AND PRACTICES	SUGGESTED LEARNING ACTIVITIES	REFERENCES AND MATERIALS
The Practice of Love 1. Thank God for the gifts of body and soul by thinking of Him often during the day.	1. Read the poem "Adam and Eve" (cf. No. **60**, p. 15). 2. Read the story of God's Love and discuss it, No. **67**, p. 18. 3. Chalk talk on the soul of man as the image of God, No. **25**, p. 28, Vol. I. 4. Draw pictures of Adam and Eve in the Garden of Paradise.	Morrow, *My Catholic Faith*, p. 35 (cf. No. **24**, p. 92). Baierl, *The Creed Explained*, p. 177 (cf. No. **11**, p. 92). Horan, *Bible Lessons* (cf. No. **3**, p. 92).
1. Grow in grace by doing kind and courteous acts for others.	1. Compare grace to an electric light. Grace: our ticket to heaven. 2. Read the poem, "Life of Grace," No. **56**, p. 18. 3. List the ways in which we can obtain and keep God's free gifts of grace.	Morrow, *My Catholic Faith*, p. 37 (cf. No. **24**, p. 92).
1. Do what is right because it pleases God who sees all and knows all.	1. Dramatize little skits showing how our conscience tells us what to do and what not to do. 2. Read and discuss the poem "Night and Day," No. **57**, p. 96 and "God's Greatness," No. **57**, p. 9. 3. Suggested Filmstrip: Creation and Fall of Man (cf. No. **67**, Unit 4).	Dennerle, *Leading the Little Ones to Christ*, p. 57 (cf. No. **14**, p. 92). Horan, *Bible Lessons*, p. 8 (cf. No. **3**, p. 92).
1. Thank your parents and teachers when they correct you or punish you because they love you and want to help you. 2. Forgive others when they hurt you and ask God to bless them, because God has been so good in forgiving you.	1. Discuss how sin displeases God by listing the punishments for the sin of Adam and Eve: Loss of grace, darkened mind, weakened will, and weakened body. 2. Discuss the promise of God's Son and His names of Jesus, Saviour, and Redeemer. 3. Discuss God's mercy toward Adam and Eve, and toward us.	Horan, *Bible Lessons*, p. 11 (cf. No. **3**, p. 92). Baierl, *The Creed Explained*, p. 209 (cf. No. **11**, p. 92). Dennerle, *Leading the Little Ones to Christ*, p. 62 (cf. No. **14**, p. 92).

THINGS TO KNOW

	CONTENT	PUPIL TEXT	CHURCH YEAR	PRAYERS AND HYMNS
1st DAY	3. God created each of us to be happy with Him in heaven by knowing, loving, and serving Him in this life. He gave me all that I have and all that I am. He wants me to live forever with Him in heaven and He gives me the means to reach this end.	Lesson 1 Questions 3, 4 Page 15	September 29 Feast of St. Michael the Archangel No. **32**, Vol. 2	Original prayers to thank God for good health and to help the sick. Mental Prayer: 1. Think of how good God has been to me. 2. Tell Him how much I love Him.
2nd DAY	4. How man's life differs from that of plants and animals: *a)* a man grows, as do plants, and he moves about and can know things through his senses, as do animals *b)* a man can, in addition, think, love, and choose *c)* a man is destined for life eternal		Month of the Holy Rosary No. **16**, p. 73 No. **57**, p. 15	"Queen of the holy Rosary, pray for us."
3rd DAY	5. How other people that God created help me: *a)* in my family		October 2 Feast of the Guardian Angels No. **57**, p. 10	Original prayers to ask God to bless my parents, brothers, and sisters.
4th DAY	*b)* in the Catholic Church: 1) Pope 2) Bishops 3) Priests 4) Sisters 5) Brothers 6) Lay Catechists 7) Jesus saves us through His Church	Lesson 4 Question 36 (21) Page 27	October 3 St. Therese (Little Flower) No. **57**, p. 12	Offer prayers today for many more priests and sisters.
5th DAY	Brief review, drill, and application to life of the basic truths learned during this 5th week.			

20

THINGS TO DO

VIRTUES AND PRACTICES	SUGGESTED LEARNING ACTIVITIES	REFERENCES AND MATERIALS
1. Take proper care of your body. 2. Love everyone because God does. 3. Learn everything God wants you to know. 4. Choose promptly what God wants.	1. Discuss health pictures to show how to take good care of our bodies. 2. Discuss pictures of people of different races and stations in life and how we must love them. 3. Read and discuss the poem, "My God and I," No. **56**, p. 1. 4. Solve problems by choosing which thing you would do from a list of things which are good and less good.	Morrow, *My Catholic Faith*, pp. 36–37 (cf. No. **24**, p. 92).

1. Choose the "High Road" of life by practicing self-control:
  a) work when you should work, play when you should play
  b) try to be friendly to everyone, even those you may not like
  c) stop play when the bell rings
	1. Chalk talk on the kinds of life, No. **25**, p. 28, Vol. I.
	2. Discuss what plants, animals, and man can do:
	  a) plants: eat, drink, grow, make seeds for other plants.
	  b) animals: in addition to doing what plants do, animals move, feel, smell, taste, touch, see, and hear
	  c) man: in addition to doing what plants and animals do, man can think, choose, love, live forever
		Morrow, *My Catholic Faith*, pp. 34–35 (cf. No. **24**, p. 92).

1. Offer to help your parents, brothers, and sisters before they ask, because God wants you to help others.	1. Collect pictures to show how our families help us. 2. Dramatize ways in which we can help the members of our family. 3. Read and discuss the poem, "Helping Others," No. **57**, p. 82.	
1. Greet priests and sisters in a friendly and helpful way because they are God's special helpers.	1. Discuss pictures of people in the Catholic Church who help us: bishops, priests, sisters, people in heaven and on earth. 2. Make a chart showing how we can help them. 3. Read and discuss the poems, "Catholic Church," and "The Catholic Child," No. **57**, pp. 40–42.	Pictures of pope, bishop, pastor.

THINGS TO KNOW

	CONTENT	PUPIL TEXT	CHURCH YEAR	PRAYERS AND HYMNS
1st DAY	c) in the community: 1) policemen 6) nurse 2) firemen 7) teacher 3) milkman 8) bus driver, 4) mailman etc. 5) doctor		October 4 St. Francis of Assisi, No. **57**, p. 13	Pray for our president and his helpers.
2nd DAY	d) in the whole world: 1) president, etc. 2) factory workers 3) farmers 4) office workers			Original prayers to our Blessed Mother for the whole world especially for Russia.
3rd DAY	6. There are some people who do not know God's plan and others who do not help carry it out: a) some have never learned the message of Christ — pagans b) some who have learned His message have forgotten it — "fallen-away Catholics"			"Dear God, help those people to know You better."
4th DAY	c) some do not use God's helps: prayer and the sacraments d) some refuse to love and serve Him e) our duty to help these people			Pray for sinners as directed by Our Lady of Fatima.
5th DAY	Brief review, drill, and application to life of the basic truths learned during this 6th week.			

THINGS TO DO

VIRTUES AND PRACTICES	SUGGESTED LEARNING ACTIVITIES	REFERENCES AND MATERIALS
1. Obey the traffic officers and patrol boys and be kind to them because they do so much to keep you safe.	1. Collect pictures of helpers in our community and discuss what they do. 2. Dramatize what these helpers do for us and what we can do for them, especially safety helpers.	
1. Be kind to all people, no matter what their race or work.	1. Discuss pictures of people from different countries, different races, and different stations in life: *a*) how they are different *b*) how they are alike *c*) how we must love them as ourselves	Pictures of Christ and His helpers.
1. Be a "Home Missionary": *a*) sacrifice by giving up candy and movies	1. Discuss how we can help those poor people: *a*) by praying for them *b*) by giving good example *c*) by sacrificing for them	
1. Pray for the missions and for more Sisters and priests to help them.	1. Organize an F.F.A. Club (Friends from Far Away).	

THINGS TO KNOW

	CONTENT	PUPIL TEXT	CHURCH YEAR	PRAYERS AND HYMNS
1st DAY	D. What we can do for God through prayer. 1. Mental prayer: A talk with my heavenly Father to thank Him for His gifts.			Mental prayer: Think of God and tell Him how good He is, how great He is, how beautiful He is, how much you love Him. Long Live Christ Our King.
2nd DAY	2. Vocal prayer: *a)* the Morning Offering: doing all for God: 1) why we should do all for God 2) how we should do all since it is for God			Teach the Morning Offering. Pupil Text — Page 4
3rd DAY	*b)* the family rosary: 1) the prayers of the rosary and the mysteries			Mental prayer: The Rosary. Moving Pictures. Make a picture of the mysteries in our minds and watch what the characters do; listen.
4th DAY	*c)* the Apostles' Creed: explanation of the vocabulary and memorization			Review the Apostles' Creed. Pupil Text — Page 3
5th DAY	Brief review, drill, and application to life of the basic truths learned during this 7th week and during this Unit.			

THINGS TO DO

VIRTUES AND PRACTICES	SUGGESTED LEARNING ACTIVITIES	REFERENCES AND MATERIALS
1. Offer prayers to God during the day to thank Him.	1. Read the poem, "A Prayer Without Words," and discuss it, No. **61**, p. 26. 2. Compare mental prayer with a beautiful dream. 3. Make a meditation with the children.	LeBuffe, *Let's Try Mental Prayer*, p. 16 (cf. No. **48**, p. 93). Thayer, *The Child on His Knees*, p. 43 (cf. No. **62**, p. 93).
1. Offer your works to God and do them as well as you can today, because God deserves your best.	1. Solve problems of how children act alone, why they do what is right or wrong, and how they do their work. Decide whether they do everything for God or not.	*The Child on His Knees*, p. 85 (see above). Morrow, *My Catholic Faith*, p. 375 (cf. No. **24**, p. 92).
1. Say the rosary with your families because God and His Mother love to hear you pray together.	1. Post a picture of a moving picture machine with a screen. Each day put a picture of one of the mysteries of the rosary on the screen. Children observe the picture so that they can make an imaginary picture of it in their minds while they pray. 2. Encourage our parents to listen to religious programs.	Cook, *The Rosary for Little Fingers* (cf. No. **44**, p. 93). Morrow, *My Catholic Faith*, p. 382 (cf. No. **24**, p. 92).
1. Thank God that you are a Catholic by telling others how good He is: *a*) a story you heard in school *b*) some blessing God gave you	1. Discuss how we got the Apostles' Creed, why we believe all it says, and why it pleases God when we say it in the rosary. 2. Explain and memorize the Apostles' Creed part by part. 3. Read and discuss poem, "Faith, Hope, and Love," No. **57**, p. 45.	Baierl, *The Creed Explained* (cf. No. **11**, p. 92). Morrow, *My Catholic Faith*, p. 4 (cf. No. **24**, p. 92).

UNIT II. *HOW SOME PEOPLE OBEYED GOD*

I. INTRODUCTION FOR THE TEACHER

The purpose of Unit II is to inculcate the spirit of obedience through a study of some models of obedience in both the Old and New Testaments. In addition the teacher will strive to develop within the child a deeper knowledge of the meaning of Advent and to give him a greater appreciation of the Nativity. (Incarnation — God becomes man.)

II. OBJECTIVES

A. To know and appreciate how many of the holy people who lived before Jesus loved and obeyed the true God.
B. To have a deep appreciation of Mary and Joseph's obedience to God.
C. To know and understand how Jesus Christ obeyed His heavenly Father in His Public Life as well as in His Passion and death.
D. To learn from the obedience of the saints how we must obey God.
E. To gain a deeper knowledge of the meaning of Advent and to instill a greater appreciation of the Nativity. (God becomes man to save us.)

III. SUBJECT MATTER

A. How the holy people who lived before Jesus teach us to obey.
B. How the Holy Family teaches us to obey.
C. How the saints teach us to obey.
D. Preparation for the coming of Jesus Christ.

A SUGGESTED DEVELOPMENT LESSON PLAN

I. SUBJECT MATTER

A. How Abraham obeyed God when it was hard (cf. p. 28, Second Day).

II. TYPE

Development.

III. OBJECTIVES

A. To know and appreciate how many of the people who lived before Jesus loved and obeyed God.

IV. SUGGESTED PROCEDURE

A. Approach

We know that there were many holy men who lived on this earth before Jesus came. These men loved God very much. They showed their love for God by obeying Him in all things.

B. Presentation

1. Leaving his homeland in obedience to God.

   Abraham was one of these holy men. God told him to leave his home and country and go into a faraway place to make a new home. This was not easy to do. Abraham obeyed God and moved into this new land. God was pleased with Abraham's obedience. He blessed Abraham and sent him a son. The little boy's name was Isaac. Abraham loved his son very much and thanked God for him.

2. His perfect obedience in willingness to sacrifice Isaac.

   One day God told Abraham to do something even harder than leaving his homeland. God wanted to test his obedience again. An angel was sent to Abraham to tell him to sacrifice his son, Isaac. This meant that Abraham was to burn his son just as he did the sheep which he offered to God. Do you think that was hard for Abraham to do? Yes, but because Abraham loved God more than he loved anyone or anything else, even his son Isaac, he was willing to obey.

   God was pleased when He saw that Abraham was really going to sacrifice Isaac. Just as Abraham was about to strike his son, an angel came and held his hand so that he could not hurt his son. The angel told Abraham that God was very pleased with his obedience, for he proved that he would obey God in all things, no matter how hard it was to do. Can you think of anything that would be harder for a father to do than to sacrifice his only son?

3. His reward: God's promise to Abraham and to his children.

   After Abraham proved that he was willing to obey God in all things, God made a wonderful promise to him. God told Abraham that he would have many children.

C. Organization

1. Who was Abraham?
2. What did God ask him to do?
3. What other hard thing did Abraham have to do?
4. Was God pleased with Abraham? Why?
5. What promise did God give to Abraham?

D. Virtues and Practice

1. Prompt obedience. Learn to obey because by doing so you imitate the Child Jesus.

E. Prayer

1. Jesus, teach me to obey when it is hard to do so.

F. Assignment

Catechism Question 45 at the end of Lesson 6 in pupil text.

V. SUGGESTED LEARNING ACTIVITIES

A. Illustrate the story of Abraham and add it to the Booklet of People who lived before Jesus.

VI. REFERENCES AND MATERIALS

A. Teacher Reference
   1. Johnson, Rev. George, *Bible Story*, pp. 18–34.
B. Children's Reference
   1. Doane, Pelagi, *A Small Child's Bible*, p. 16.
   2. *Jesus Comes*, Lesson 6.

THINGS TO KNOW

	CONTENT	PUPIL TEXT	CHURCH YEAR	PRAYERS AND HYMNS

1st DAY	A. How some persons who lived before Jesus taught us to obey.
	
	1. How Noe obeyed the true God:
	
	   a) the building of the Ark in obedience to God's command
	   b) Noe's reward: the remaking of the human race
		Lesson 5
		Questions 38, 39
		Page 30
				"O Lord, protect all of us, Your children, now and forever." Amen.

2nd DAY	2. How Abraham obeyed God when it was hard:
	
	   a) leaving his homeland in obedience to God
	   b) his perfect obedience in willingness to sacrifice Isaac
	   c) his reward: God's promise to him and to his children
		Lesson 6
		Question 45
		Page 32
				"Sweet Jesus, help us to prove our love for You by obeying You."

3rd DAY	3. How Moses obeyed God's call: Story of the Burning Bush:
	
	   a) what God told Moses to do
	   b) how God helped Moses to obey
		Lesson 7
		Question 50
		Page 34
				Mental Prayer:
				
				1. Think of God.
				2. Listen for things He would like you to do today.

4th DAY	4. How Samuel obeyed the voice of God:
	
	   a) his courage in obeying God's will
	   b) how he answered God's voice
	   c) how he was made a leader of his people as a reward for his obedience
	   d) duties of parents to punish the wrongs of their children
		Lesson 8
		Questions 53–55
		Page 36
		Questions 56–58
		Page 36
			Last Sunday of October
			
			Christ the King
				"Dear Lord, help me to know Your will."

5th DAY	Brief review, drill, and application to life of the basic truths learned during this 8th week.			

THINGS TO DO

VIRTUES AND PRACTICES	SUGGESTED LEARNING ACTIVITIES	REFERENCES AND MATERIALS
The Practice of Fortitude 1. Do what God wants today when He speaks to you through your parents, teachers, or others who take His place.	1. Attentive listening to the story of Noe and the Ark in preparation for class discussion. 2. Discuss the picture of the story. 3. Begin a frieze or booklet to show the obedience of people who lived before Jesus. 4. Read and discuss the poem, "Noe and the Ark," No. **58**.*	Doanne, *A Small Child's Bible,* p. 12 (cf. No. **1**, p. 92).* Horan, *Bible Lessons,* p. 16 (cf. No. **3**, p. 92).*
God blesses obedience: 1. Go to bed when told, even if it means you must leave in the middle of a good radio or television program. 2. Help your parents by doing jobs you don't like, such as washing the dishes or emptying the garbage.	1. Discuss the picture of Abraham's sacrifice. 2. Discuss times when it takes courage for us to obey. 3. Add this picture to the frieze or booklet.	Horan, *Bible Lessons,* p. 30 (cf. No. **3**, p. 92).* Doanne, *A Small Child's Bible,* p. 16 (cf. No. **1**, p. 92).*
1. Ask God to help you do what He wants when you feel afraid; when you don't think that you can do it; or when you don't like to do it — because God is good and wants to help you.	1. Compose a chart showing how Moses obeyed God's call. 2. Draw a picture of Moses as he awakened from sleep to obey God's call and add it to the frieze or booklet.	Horan, *Bible Lessons,* p. 63 (cf. No. **3**, p. 92).* Doanne, *A Small Child's Bible,* p. 34 (cf. No. **1**, p. 92).*
1. Answer your parents and teachers in a pleasant and willing way when they ask you to do something, for example, say "Surely" or "I'll be glad to," because they take God's place.	1. Compare Samuel's answer to God with our answers to our parents. 2. Make a picture of Samuel for the frieze or booklet.	Horan, *Bible Lessons,* p. 93 (cf. No. **3**, p. 92).* Doanne, *A Small Child's Bible,* p. 52 (cf. No. **1**, p. 92).*

* For all keyed references in boldface type, see Teacher Bibliography, pp. 92–93, at end of this Teacher's Manual.

THINGS TO KNOW

	CONTENT	PUPIL TEXT	CHURCH YEAR	PRAYERS AND HYMNS
1st DAY	(All Saints' Day) 1. Saints are people who did God's will on earth. 2. Canonized saints: saints we know by name. 3. Uncanonized saints: saints that are unknown.		November 1 All Saints' Day No. **57**, p. 16	"Blessed be God in His angels and in His saints."

2nd DAY	(All Souls' Day)
	
	1. Purgatory
	2. How the souls suffer in purgatory
	3. How we can help them:
	  a) prayer
	  b) sacrifices
			November 2
			
			All Souls' Day No. **57**, p. 19
				"Eternal rest grant unto them, O Lord; and let perpetual light shine upon them. May they rest in peace." Amen. (No. 582; 300 days.)

3rd DAY	B. How the Holy Family Taught Us to Obey
	
	1. The obedience of Mary and the Son of God at the Annunciation:
	  a) Mary's willingness to help carry out God's plan
	  b) Mary's willingness to accept sorrow
	  c) how God the Son became poor and small when He obeyed His Father and became man
		Lesson 9
		Question 59
		Page 42
		Questions 60–62
		Page 42
				"Mary, dear Mother, help us to obey."

4th DAY	2. The obedience of Jesus Christ, Mary and Joseph at the Nativity:
	  a) the journey to Bethlehem: obedience to the civil law
	  b) the birth of Jesus
	  c) the Circumcision: obedience to the law of Moses
	  d) the Presentation: obedience to the law of Moses
		Lesson 9
		Questions 63, 64, 65
		Pages 42–43
				Offer prayers for those who make the laws of our country. Pray for the priests and sisters who help us.

5th DAY	Brief review, drill, and application to life of the basic truths learned during this 9th week.			

45
(or halloween)

26

THINGS TO DO

VIRTUES AND PRACTICES	SUGGESTED LEARNING ACTIVITIES	REFERENCES AND MATERIALS
1. Practice the outstanding virtues of your patron saint.	1. Read and discuss stories about our patron saints, No. **31**, Vols. I, II, III. 2. Dramatize an incident in the lives of a few of our patron saints. 3. Read and discuss the poem, "All Saints," No. **57**, p. 16.	Morrow, *My Catholic Faith*, pp. 188–189 (cf. No. **24**, p. 92).
1. Make a little sacrifice for the poor souls. 2. Assist at Holy Mass for the Poor Souls. 3. Say little ejaculations during the day for the Poor Souls.	1. Discuss the ways of making little sacrifices for the poor souls. 2. Make a class chart of "How I Can Help the Poor Souls." 3. Read and discuss the poem, "All Souls' Day," No. **57**, p. 19. 4. Read stories about the Poor Souls.	Morrow, *My Catholic Faith*, p. 149 (cf. No. **24**, p. 93).
The Practice of Justice 1. Carry out God's plan right away when your parents, priests, or teachers tell you to do something. Obey cheerfully when it means that you must give up something you like to do, because Jesus gave up many lovely things when He was on earth.	1. Dramatize the Story of the Annunciation, p. 88. 2. Read and discuss the poem, "Hail Full of Grace," No. **57**, p. 55.	Morrow, *My Catholic Faith*, p. 60 (cf. No. **24**, p. 92).

1. Be good Americans by keeping the laws of your city and have respect for the policemen, school guards, and other people who have charge of you.
2. Be good members of your Church by keeping its laws:
  a) assist at Mass on Sundays and holydays
  b) keep from eating meat on Friday
  c) support the Church
	1. Make a movie showing how we can be good citizens.
	2. List some laws of our city regarding safety and health.
	3. List some ways in which we can obey our pastor and priests.
	4. Read the story, "Presentation," and discuss it, No. **1**, p. 96.
		Horan, *Bible Lessons*, p. 141 (cf. No. **3**, p. 92).
		
		Morrow, *My Catholic Faith*, p. 63 (cf. No. **24**, p. 92).

THINGS TO KNOW

	CONTENT	PUPIL TEXT	CHURCH YEAR	PRAYERS AND HYMNS
1st DAY	3. The obedience of the Holy Family in the Flight into Egypt and the return: *a*) Joseph's obedience to the Angel: in Bethlehem — in Egypt *b*) Mary's obedience to Joseph *c*) Jesus Christ's obedience to Mary and to Joseph			Say the prayer, "Angel of God" before taking long trips and when: 1. Going to or from school 2. Going for a ride 3. Going to the store
2nd DAY	4. The obedience at Nazareth: *a*) Jesus and Mary obeyed Joseph as the head of the family *b*) the perfect obedience of Jesus Christ to Mary and to Joseph			Mental Prayer: 1. Make a picture in our minds of the Holy Family. 2. Watch how they obeyed. 3. Ask them to help us and our families to obey. 4. Promise to obey, No. **48**, p. 21.
3rd DAY	5. The obedience of Jesus Christ at the Feast of the Passover when He was twelve years old: *a*) to His heavenly Father: His Stay in the Temple *b*) to His Mother and foster father: "He was subject to them"			"Jesus, teach me how to pray." Pray to Jesus to help us to be brave enough to do what is right.
4th DAY				
5th DAY	Brief review, drill, and application to life of the basic truths learned during this 10th week.			

THINGS TO DO

VIRTUES AND PRACTICES	SUGGESTED LEARNING ACTIVITIES	REFERENCES AND MATERIALS
1. Make sacrifices to be obedient because God blesses us: *a)* take care of your little brother or sister even when you would rather play *b)* get up promptly in the morning when mother calls	1. Discuss the reason why Joseph obeyed the angel; why Jesus obeyed Mary and Joseph and why Mary obeyed Joseph. 2. Make a chart entitled, "How I can be a Good Member of my Family."	Johnson, *The Bible Story,* p. 156 (cf. No. **4**, p. 92). Morrow, *My Catholic Faith,* p. 63 (cf. No. **24**, p. 92).
1. Do what you are told even if you think you know better, because Jesus did this. 2. Ask your parents sometimes what they would like you to do or what they think is better for you to do.	1. Compare the activities of the Holy Family with those of ours. 2. Make charts entitled, "How the Holy Family obeyed God" and "How Our Family Obeys God." 3. Read and discuss the poem, "Jesus at Nazareth," No. **60**, p. 30.	Morrow, *My Catholic Faith,* p. 64 (cf. No. **24**, p. 92).
1. Obey God first when you must choose between what God tells you and what others tell you: *a)* when someone tells you to stay away from Mass on Sundays or holydays *b)* when someone gives you meat on Fridays, etc.	1. Read and discuss the poem, "Christ in the Temple," No. **60**, p. 26. 2. Discuss how obedience to God comes first and the times when we would have to obey God before all others. 3. Story of Eleazar (Maccabeus).	Horan, *Bible Lessons,* p. 146 (cf. No. **3**, p. 92). Johnson, *The Bible Story,* pp. 157–161 (cf. No. **4**, p. 92).
1. Obey your parents promptly at all times because Jesus did this.	1. Dramatize what you would say and how you would act if others made fun of your religion or of you because you did right.	

THINGS TO KNOW

	CONTENT	PUPIL TEXT	CHURCH YEAR	PRAYERS AND HYMNS

1st DAY	6. Jesus' obedience to His heavenly Father during His Public Life:
	
	a) in the teachings He gave through parables:
	  1) Good Samaritan
	  2) Good Shepherd
	  3) Sowing of the Seed
			November 21
			
			Presentation of the Blessed Virgin Mary
				Mental Prayer:
				
				1. Picture Jesus teaching the people.
				2. Ask Jesus to help me do the things He taught.

2nd DAY	*b*) in His Miracles:
	
	  1) Storm at Sea
	  2) Daughter of Jairus
	  3) Cure of Ten Lepers
	  4) Draught of Fishes
	  5) Cure of Blind and Sick
			November 22
			
			Feast of St. Cecilia
				Mental Prayer:
				
				1. Picture Jesus working one of His miracles.
				2. Thank Jesus for His goodness to us.
				3. Praise Him for His power, No. **48**, p. 20.

3rd DAY	*c*) in His Journeys:
	
	  1) to Galilee
	  2) to Capharnaum
	  3) to Naim
	  4) to Bethany
				Ask Jesus to help us to do our duties well.

4th DAY	7. The obedience of Jesus Christ in His Passion and Death.			Original prayers for sins: "Father, forgive them, for they do not know what they are doing." Original Acts of Contrition.
5th DAY	Brief review, drill, and application to life of the basic truths learned during this 11th week.			

THINGS TO DO

VIRTUES AND PRACTICES	SUGGESTED LEARNING ACTIVITIES	REFERENCES AND MATERIALS
1. Make sacrifices to be obedient, since by obedience you become pleasing to God: a) take care of your little brother or sister b) be attentive in school at all times because your teacher takes God's place	1. Show a picture of a parable and call upon individual children to tell the story it calls to mind. 2. Draw pictures to illustrate the different parables. 3. Read and discuss the story, "The Presentation," No. **16**.	Horan, *Bible Lessons*, pp. 191–196 (cf. No. **3**, p. 92). Lloyd, *Jesus Teaching*, pp. 157–214 (cf. No. **22**, p. 92).
1. Be thoughtful and attentive to the needs of others at home, at school, and at play.	1. Dramatize a favorite miracle. 2. Read and discuss the poem, "St. Cecilia," cf. No. **57**, p. 22.	Horan, *Bible Lessons*, pp. 168–170–184 (cf. No. **3**, p. 92).
1. Do the right thing, at the right time, and in the right way because the chance may never come again: a) attend Mass on Sundays and holydays even when it is hard to do so b) be in school on time c) do not let little hardships keep you away (rain or snow)	1. Discuss pictures of Jesus during His Public Life doing the duties given Him by His heavenly Father. 2. Read stories that tell about some of these duties.	Johnson, *The Bible Story*, pp. 169–189 (cf. No. **4**, p. 92).
1. Take the pain or suffering that God may send you today, and offer it to Him for sinners: a) the pain of keeping good posture all day b) the sacrifice of being quiet at the right time	1. Flash picture of the Passion and Death of Jesus on the screen. 2. Read stories from library readers on the Passion and Death of Jesus, No. **12**, Bk. 6. 3. Read and discuss the Poem, "The Agony," No. **57**, p. 57.	Horan, *Bible Lessons*, p. 211 (cf. No. **3**, p. 92).

THINGS TO KNOW

	CONTENT	PUPIL TEXT	CHURCH YEAR	PRAYERS AND HYMNS

1st DAY	C. How the saints taught us to obey:
	
	1. St. Matthew: his obedience to Christ's call
	2. St. Peter: his obedience to Christ's commands:
	   a) to leave his fishing nets
	   b) to let down his nets
				Pray for vocations.
				
				"St. Peter, pray for us and for the whole Catholic Church."

2nd DAY	3. St. Paul: his obedience to God's directions			"St. Paul, pray for us and for the whole world."
3rd DAY	4. The children of Fatima: their obedience to our Blessed Mother			"O my Jesus, we offer this for Your Love, the conversion of sinners, and for all the wrongs committed against the Immaculate Heart of Mary." (Prayer taught to children by Our Lady of Fatima.)
4th DAY	5. St. Bernadette: her obedience to our Blessed Mother Mary at Lourdes			"O Mary, conceived without sin, pray for us who have recourse to thee." (No. 357; 300 days.)
5th DAY	Brief review, drill, and application to life of the basic truths learned during this 12th week.			

THINGS TO DO

VIRTUES AND PRACTICES	SUGGESTED LEARNING ACTIVITIES	REFERENCES AND MATERIALS
1. Obey your parents because they take God's place and know what is best for you. 2. Offer to help with little duties at home without being asked.	1. Dramatize the call of St. Matthew, No. **61**, p. 49. 2. Discuss how God calls some boys and girls to follow Him in a special way and become priests and sisters. 3. Draw a picture of St. Peter obeying the command of Jesus to let down the nets or to leave his nets.	Doanne, *Small Children's Bible*, p. 106 (cf. No. **1**, p. 92). Horan, *Bible Lesson*, p. 155 (cf. No. **3**, p. 92).
1. Obey all those who are in charge of you, since they take the place of God: *a)* your mothers and fathers *b)* the pastor and his assistants *c)* the sisters and teachers at school *d)* the policeman on the corner	1. Dramatize the story of the conversion of St. Paul or have a radio program, No. **31**, Vol. 1. 2. Discuss how sufferings helped St. Paul and how they can help us to love and obey God more.	Morrow, *My Catholic Faith*, p. 80 (cf. No. **24**, p. 92).
1. Make sacrifices that Mary asked: *a)* first Saturday Communion (Spiritual Communion) *b)* daily family rosary *c)* do something hard each day	1. Observe the film strip on Our Lady of Fatima or read the story, "Our Lady of Fatima," No. **39**. 2. Dramatize what Mary's wishes were and how we can carry them out. 3. Sing the song, "Our Lady of Fatima." 4. Read and discuss poem, "Mary's Obedience," No. **61**, p. 131.	
1. Give up comfort and pleasure to help: *a)* take care of the baby so that mother can go to Confession or Holy Mass *b)* wash the dishes so that the family can say the rosary together	1. Read and discuss the poem, "Bernadette," No. **61**, p. 131. 2. Sing the hymn, "Immaculate Mother" (Lourdes Hymn).	

THINGS TO KNOW

	CONTENT	PUPIL TEXT	CHURCH YEAR	PRAYERS AND HYMNS
1st DAY	D. Preparation for the Coming of Jesus Christ (at appropriate time): 1. Instruction on Advent			"Come, O come, Emmanuel" "Come, O come, Lord Jesus, Come."
2nd DAY	(St. Nicholas) 1. The Saint now called Santa Claus 2. His kindness and generosity to the poor		December 6 St. Nicholas	Original Prayers to St. Nicholas (Example) "St. Nicholas, lover of little children, pray for us."
3rd DAY	(Immaculate Conception of the Blessed Virgin Mary) 1. Mary was free from original sin 2. How God prepared Mary to be His Mother	Lesson 4 Question 37 Page 27	December 8 Immaculate Conception of the Blessed Virgin Mary	Review "O Mary, conceived without sin, pray for us who have recourse to thee." (No. 357; 300 days.)
	Brief review, drill, and application to life of the basic truths learned during this 13th week.			

4th DAY	Direct Preparation for Christmas
	1. Nativity Stories:
	  a) the message of the archangel Gabriel to Mary
	  b) the Visitation: Mary visits Zachary and Elizabeth
	  c) the Birth of Jesus at Bethlehem
	  d) the adoration of the shepherds
	  e) the coming of the Magi
			December 25
			
			The Birth of Jesus Christ
			Christmas Day
				Original prayers to the Christ Child
				
				"Glory to God in the highest and on earth peace to men of good will."

5th DAY	Brief review, drill, and application to life of the basic truths learned during this 14th week, and during this unit.			

THINGS TO DO

VIRTUES AND PRACTICES	SUGGESTED LEARNING ACTIVITIES	REFERENCES AND MATERIALS
1. Be as patient as the people in the Old Testament: a) don't complain when things go wrong b) don't tattle c) wait until it's your turn to talk	1. Make an Advent wreath. 2. Draw practices from a box or receive a letter each day from Jesus. 3. Save straws for the crib. (Children put pieces of straw in a box for good acts.)	Horan, *Bible Lessons,* p. 131 (cf. No. **3**, p. 92). Baierl, *The Creed Explained,* p. 231 (cf. No. **11**, p. 92).
1. Be kind and generous to your playmates because St. Nicholas was especially kind to little children: a) share your toys with others b) help poor boys and girls by giving to the missions	1. Read and discuss the story of St. Nicholas. 2. Dramatize the story, "St. Nicholas," No. **29**, p. 60.	
1. Show your love for God's Mother: a) assist at Holy Mass b) pray with reverence and devotion as Mary did	1. Learn and recite as a choral poem, "Mary Immaculate," No. **61**, p. 42. 2. Compose a letter to Mary telling her how you will try to imitate her. 3. Read story of "Immaculate Conception," No. **16**.	Morrow, *My Catholic Faith,* pp. 41, 239 (cf. No. **24**, p. 92).
1. Prepare for the coming of Jesus on Christmas Day: a) be reverent and devout while praying b) share with visitors: toys, books, "goodies," etc. c) give up something you like and offer this sacrifice to Jesus	1. Read and discuss the poem, "Hail Full of Grace," No. **57**, p. 55. 2. Write a letter to the Christ Child. 3. Dramatize the story of Christmas. 4. Read poems on the Christmas Story, No. **57**, pp. 30–38. 5. Prepare a gift or card for our parents for Christmas.	Baierl, *The Creed Explained,* p. 244 (cf. No. **11**, p. 92). Horan, *Bible Lessons,* p. 137 cf. No. **3**, p. 92). Morrow, *My Catholic Faith,* pp. 60, 62 (cf. No. **24**, p. 92).

UNIT III. *HOW WE SHOULD OBEY GOD*

I. INTRODUCTION FOR THE TEACHER

This unit presents the Commandments as a divinely revealed code of morality which the Church teaches men in order to help them gain eternal life. The teacher will, therefore, endeavor to acquaint the child with the proper knowledge of these laws and to develop in him a right conscience toward sin as well as a realization that these laws are a part of God's plan to help him gain heaven.

II. OBJECTIVES

A. To gain an understanding of how we can love and serve God by keeping His laws.

B. To realize that God gave us these laws to help us gain heaven.

C. To learn what these laws command and what they forbid.

D. To develop in the child a right conscience toward sin.

E. To understand that the laws of the Church are also part of God's plan to help us gain heaven.

F. To realize that we deserve God's punishment if we fail to keep His Laws.

III. SUBJECT MATTER

A. Obedience to God's laws: How we can love and adore God by keeping His first three laws.

B. Obedience to God's laws: How God's laws help us to love our neighbor as ourselves.

A SUGGESTED DEVELOPMENT LESSON PLAN

I. SUBJECT MATTER

A. God's Third Commandment: Assistance at Holy Mass on Sundays and holydays (cf. p. 43, Third Day).

II. TYPE

Development

III. OBJECTIVES

A. To realize how we can honor God in a special way on Sundays and holydays.

B. To learn what the Third Commandment prescribes.

C. To help the child grasp the seriousness of breaking the Third Commandment.

D. To realize that this law of the Church is a part of God's plan to help us to gain heaven.

IV. SUGGESTED PROCEDURE

A. Approach

Last week we learned that the first three commandments tell us how to love and adore God. In the First Commandment, God tells us to pray to Him and to adore Him. In what way does the Second Commandment help us to love God? Discuss. Today we are going to learn what God wants us to do in order to keep the Third Commandment.

B. Presentation

1. In the Third Commandment God tells us to keep all Sundays and holydays holy.

   a) Offer the Mass with the priest.

   Jesus pleased His heavenly Father when He died on the cross. By His death, Jesus showed His love for all men by rewinning for them friendship with His Father. The Mass is the same sacrifice as that which Jesus offered on the cross.

   The biggest thing we can do is to offer the Mass with the priest. In doing this, we offer Jesus to God the Father. He wants us to offer His Son to Him every day. He commands us to do this every Sunday and every holyday. Assisting at Mass on Sunday and holydays is the best way to keep these days holy.

   b) Say extra prayers.

   Besides doing what God commands us to do, there are other ways of keeping Sunday holy. We please God when we say extra prayers. Prayer is talking to God. Sunday is a day of leisure. We don't work or play as we do on other days of the week. Do you think it would be hard to find time for extra prayers on Sunday? Discuss.

   c) Attending Benediction.

   In many parishes the service known as "Benediction of the Blessed Sacrament" takes place on Sundays. It takes place either after one of the Masses or in the evening. In it, the priest blesses the people with the Blessed Sacrament. The Blessed Sacrament is another way of saying the Sacrament of the Holy

Eucharist. We know that the Blessed Sacrament is Jesus. So we say that Jesus gives us His blessing when we attend Benediction. We should always want this blessing. Would you give up the blessing of Jesus for some little thing? Discuss.

d) Read something holy.

Reading something holy is another way to spend God's day. Everyone has time for reading on Sunday. Why not read a holy story? In the bookrack in the rear of the church are many children's books about Jesus, His Blessed Mother, and His friends the saints. Ask for one of these for a gift sometime. Stories like these fill our minds with good thoughts. Then it will be easy to think of God. God wants us to think of Him often and especially on His day.

e) Do something kind for someone.

Why not try to do something kind for someone? We can always find someone who needs our help. Perhaps Mother is drying the dishes, or the baby is in mischief, and needs our help. It won't be hard to give help if we try to look for something kind to do. You will find many kind things to do for others. A kind act will help us to spend the day as God wishes us to.

C. Organization

1. What is the Third Commandment of God?
2. What does the Third Commandment tell us to do?
3. What else should I do to keep Sunday holy?

D. Virtues and Practices

I will show my love for God's Third Commandment by assisting at Mass reverently on Sundays.

I will assist at Mass in the very best way I can. — I will use my prayer book.

E. Prayers and Hymns

Let us think of a prayer in which we can tell God that we do want to keep His day holy because he wishes it so.

Suggestion: Dear God, help me to always go to Mass on Sunday because that is the best way to keep your day holy.

F. Assignment

Catechism Questions 77, 78, 79 at the end of Lesson 12.

V. SUGGESTED ACTIVITIES (use only the one you have time for)

1. Make a chart showing the time of Sunday Masses, stressing the time children should be there.
2. Make an individual booklet illustrating the different ways of keeping Sunday holy — starting with the most important.

VI. REFERENCES AND MATERIALS

Teacher:

Heeg, Rev. Aloysius, *The Illustrated Catechism*, Part II, p. 18.

Morrow, Rev. Louis, *My Catholic Faith*, p. 202, 286.

Pupil:

Jesus Comes, Lesson 12.

THINGS TO KNOW

	CONTENT	PUPIL TEXT	CHURCH YEAR	PRAYERS AND HYMNS
1st DAY	A. Obedience to God's laws: How we can love and adore God by keeping His first three laws. 1. God has helped us to know what He wants us to do by giving us His laws: *a)* by giving each of us a conscience whereby we can know right from wrong *b)* by putting these laws on tablets of stone			"Come Holy Ghost, help me to know what is right." "Thy Will be done."
2nd DAY	2. God's First Commandment: Prayer and worship of God alone: *a)* in this law God tells us to pray: 1) the meaning of prayer 2) kinds of prayer: (*a*) to adore God (*b*) to thank God (*c*) to ask God (*d*) to tell God our sorrow for our sins	Lesson 10 Questions 71, 72 Page 47		1. Original prayers to adore God, thank God, and ask God, and tell Him of our sorrow. 2. *Mental Prayer*, LeBuffe, **48**, p. 13.
3rd DAY	3) times to pray: (*a*) in the morning (*b*) at night (*c*) during the day — at meals (*d*) in times of temptation		January 6 The Epiphany	"All for Thee, Most Sacred Heart of Jesus."
4th DAY	*b)* this law forbids: 1) missing morning or night prayers for a long time through laziness, shame, etc. 2) purposely thinking of other things while praying 3) purposely attending Protestant church services	Lesson 10 Question 73 Page 47	First Sunday after the Epiphany Feast of the Holy Family	"Jesus, teach me how to pray." Original prayers for the spread of the true Church.
5th DAY	Brief review, drill, and application to life of basic truths learned during this 15th week.			

THINGS TO DO

VIRTUES AND PRACTICES	SUGGESTED LEARNING ACTIVITIES	REFERENCES AND MATERIALS
Practice of Faith Acknowledge God as your Lord and Master, and the Lord of all good. Make sacrifices for pagans so that they will know God's laws.	1. Discuss practical problems on the actions of children to find out whether or not they follow their consciences. 2. Read story "Eddie Cloud," No. **12**, Bk. 1, p. 71.* "Magic Shield," No. **27**, p. 80. "Ships that Ran Away," No. **12**, Bk. 3, p. 106. 3. Make a chart showing the two tables of God. 4. Read the poem, "The Ten Commandments," No. **57**, p. 48.*	
1. Say ejaculations today that will tell God that you adore Him, thank Him, ask Him for blessings, and tell Him of your sorrow for your sins.	1. Read stories: "Lost in the Woods" "Saving Light" "Thanksgiving," No. **12**, Bk. 2, p. 21.* "The Lepers," No. **12**, Bk. 3, p. 70.*	Schumacher, *I Teach Catechism*, pp. 155–161, Vol. 1 (cf. No. **10**, p. 92).*
1. Be faithful in saying your prayers at these times because Jesus prayed when He lived on earth.	1. Discuss pictures of children praying at these times. 2. Read poems: "My Visits," No. **57**, p. 4.* "A Child's Prayer," No. **60**, p. 93.* 3. Compare the times Jesus prayed with the times that we pray. 4. Tell or read stories about prayer, No. **12**, Bk. 1, pp. 61–68.*	Schumacher, *I Teach Catechism*, Vol. 1, pp. 52–61 (cf. No. **10**, p. 98).* Morrow, *My Catholic Faith*, pp. 372–377 (cf. No. **24**, p. 99).*

1. Pray at the right time and in the right way:
  a) even when you are tired
  b) even when others are with you
  c) with love and devotion
2. Help others learn about the Catholic Church because it was started by Jesus:
  a) tell others about the Church
  b) be a good Catholic
  c) invite others to visit Jesus in the tabernacle
	1. Discuss ways and means of remembering to say our morning and night prayers, No. **12**, Bk. 1, pp. 27–95–70.
	2. Discuss how we can distinguish Catholic churches from other churches.
	3. Draw pictures of a Catholic church showing the signs, No. **25**, p. 186.*
	4. Discuss reasons why we should not attend Protestant churches and why we should invite others to our church.
		Morrow, *My Catholic Faith*, p. 186 (cf. No. **24**, p. 99).*

* For all keyed references in boldface type, see Teacher Bibliography, pp. 92–93, at end of this Teacher's Manual.

48

THINGS TO KNOW

	CONTENT	PUPIL TEXT	CHURCH YEAR	PRAYERS AND HYMNS

1st DAY	3. God's Second Commandment: Reverence for God's holy name:
	
	  a) in this law God tells us to use His name in the right way
	  b) in this law God tells us to speak about and act with respect toward holy persons, holy places, and holy things
		Lesson 11
		Questions 74, 75
		Page 49
				Say the Divine Praises. (No. 696, 3 years.)
				
				"Dear Jesus, help me to love all holy things."

2nd DAY	*c*) this law forbids:
	
	    1) using the holy names of God carelessly or in anger
	    2) speaking about or acting disrespectfully of holy persons, holy places, and holy things
		Lesson 11
		Question 76
		Page 49
				"Dear Jesus, I love Your Holy Name."
				
				"Jesus" (No. 113, 300 days).

3rd DAY	4. God's Third Commandment: Assistance at Holy Mass on Sundays and holydays:
	  a) in this law God tells us to keep Sundays and holydays holy:
	    1) offer the Mass with the priest
	    2) say extra prayers
	    3) attend benediction
	    4) read something holy
	    5) do something kind for someone
		Lesson 12
		Questions 77, 78, 79
		Page 52
			January 13
			The Baptism of Our Lord
				Original Prayers
				
				"Dear Jesus, help me to keep Your day holy."

4th DAY	*b*) this law forbids:
	
	    1) missing Mass on Sundays and holydays *through our own fault*
	    2) coming late to Mass on these days through our own fault
	    3) misbehaving in church
	    4) doing work that is not necessary
		Lesson 12
		Question 80
		Page 52
				Original Prayers
				
				"Dear Jesus, give me the grace never to miss Mass through my own fault."

5th DAY	Brief review, drill, and application to life of basic truths learned during this 16th week.			

THINGS TO DO

VIRTUES AND PRACTICES	SUGGESTED LEARNING ACTIVITIES	REFERENCES AND MATERIALS
Practice of Hope 1. Bow your head when you say or hear the name of Jesus. 2. Encourage your father to join the Holy Name Society. 3. Be reverent toward holy persons, places, and things because they belong to God in a special way.	1. Discuss the different names of God. 2. Discuss the purpose of the Holy Name Society. 3. Read and discuss the "Divine Praises." 4. Have a boy pretend he is passing a church, meeting a priest or Sister. 5. Discuss pictures of children who are genuflecting. 6. Practice genuflecting with the class.	Schumacher, *I Teach Catechism*, Vol. 1, pp. 161–165 (cf. No. **10**, p. 92). Morrow, *My Catholic Faith*, pp. 198–199 (cf. No. **24**, p. 92).
1. Secretly whisper a little prayer when you hear someone use God's name in the wrong way to make up for the injury done to Jesus. 2. When others make fun of holy things show that you do not like it by not laughing and telling them it is wrong.	1. Discuss the story "The Boy and the Nails," No. **12**, Bk. 1, p. 30. 2. Discuss and illustrate ways of helping ourselves to overcome bad habits.	Schumacher, *I Teach Catechism*, Vol. 1, pp. 161–165 (cf. No. **10**, p. 92). Morrow, *My Catholic Faith*, pp. 198–199 (cf. No. **24**, p. 92).
Practice of Love 1. Show your love for God's Third Commandment by: *a*) being devout and reverent at Sunday Mass *b*) getting to Sunday Mass on time	1. Make an individual booklet illustrating the different ways of keeping Sunday holy. 2. Make a chart of the time of Sunday Masses, stressing the time children should be there.	Schumacher, *I Teach Catechism*, Vol. 1, pp. 165–169 (cf. No. **10**, p. 92). Morrow, *My Catholic Faith*, pp. 202–286 (cf. No. **24**, p. 92).
1. Invite others to come to Mass with you. 2. Help yourself and others to love and honor God by behaving well in church. 3. Help mother and father on Saturday so that they do not have to work on Sunday.	1. Discuss ways we can be late through our own faults: walking too slowly, not leaving on time, stopping to play. 2. Discuss ways we can miss Mass through our own fault. 3. Dramatize behavior in church: proper genuflection, sitting, kneeling, etc. 4. Discuss unnecessary work with the children.	Schumacher, *I Teach Catechism*, Vol. 1, pp. 165–169 (cf. No. **10**, p. 92). Morrow, *My Catholic Faith*, pp. 202–286 (cf. No. **24**, p. 92).

49

THINGS TO KNOW

	CONTENT	PUPIL TEXT	CHURCH YEAR	PRAYERS AND HYMNS
1st DAY	B. Obedience to God's laws: How God's laws help us to love our neighbor as ourselves. 1. God's Fourth Commandment: Obedience to our parents and to all those who take their place: *a*) in this law God tells us to love, honor, obey, help, and pray for our parents	Lesson 13 Questions 81, 82 Page 54		"Dear God, help me to love, honor, obey, and help my parents."
2nd DAY				
3rd DAY	*b*) this law forbids: 1) disobeying our parents, teachers, and those who take their place 2) talking back to our parents 3) being mean toward our parents or those placed over us; saying unkind things about them 4) making fun of our parents and of old people	Lesson 13 Question 83 Page 54		Mental prayer: 1. Picture in our minds the Christ Child obeying His blessed mother and foster father. 2. Promise Jesus to do as He did, No. **48**, p. 20.
4th DAY				
5th DAY	Brief review, drill, and application to life of basic truths learned during this 17th week.			

THINGS TO DO

VIRTUES AND PRACTICES	SUGGESTED LEARNING ACTIVITIES	REFERENCES AND MATERIALS
Spiritual and Corporal Works of Mercy 1. Obey your parents and those in charge of you promptly and cheerfully because they take God's place.	1. Dramatize how children can please God by obeying their parents or those in charge of them: *a)* do the dishes *b)* go to the store *c)* sweep the floor *d)* watch the baby	Morrow, *My Catholic Faith*, p. 206 (cf. No. **24**, p. 92). Schumacher, *I Teach Catechism*, Vol. 1, pp. 171–177 (cf. No. **10**, p. 92).
1. Answer your parents and older people in a kind and loving manner even when it is hard for you to do so.	1. Children draw pictures and discuss different ways in which they can be kind to their parents and to old people: *a)* offer to be helpful to old people *b)* go on an errand for mother *c)* offer old people a seat on the bus	Morrow, *My Catholic Faith*, p. 206 (cf. No. **24**, p. 92). Schumacher, *I Teach Catechism*, Vol. 1, pp. 171–177 (cf. No. **10**, p. 92).

THINGS TO KNOW

	CONTENT	PUPIL TEXT	CHURCH YEAR	PRAYERS AND HYMNS

1st DAY	2. God's Fifth Command: Being kind to everyone:
	
	a) in this law God tells us:
	  1) to show our love for others in the family, the school, and in the community
	  2) to help others do what is right
	  3) to take proper care of our own health and safety and that of others
		Lesson 14
		Questions 84, 85
		Page 56
			January 21
			Feast of St. Agnes
				"Dear Jesus, help me to be kind to everyone."
				
				Pray for the safety of our policemen, firemen, and others whose lives are in danger.

2nd DAY				

3rd DAY	*b*) this law forbids:
	
	  1) being angry
	  2) being stubborn
	  3) being mean to others
	  4) looking down on others
	  5) trying to get even with others
	  6) fighting and quarreling
	  7) treating animals with cruelty
	  8) teaching others to do wrong
	  9) giving bad example
		Lesson 14
		Question 86
		Page 56
				"Dear Jesus, make our hearts like yours."
				
				Prayer for those who have hurt us or been unkind to us.

4th DAY				
5th DAY	Brief review, drill, and application to life of basic truths learned during this 18th week.			

THINGS TO DO

VIRTUES AND PRACTICES	SUGGESTED LEARNING ACTIVITIES	REFERENCES AND MATERIALS

1. Be kind and thoughtful of others at home, at school, and on the playground because God made them.
2. Practice the safety rules and laws that you have learned at home and in school because they were made for your own good.
	1. Follow the good example of members of our families.
	2. Illustrate some ways in which we can look after the health and safety of others:
	  a) at home
	  b) in school
	  c) in the neighborhood
	    No. **12**, Bk. 3, pp. 78, 110.
	3. Suggested Filmstrip: St. Agnes (cf. No. **72**, Lives of the Saints).
		Schumacher, *I Teach Catechism*, Vol. 1, pp. 177–182 (cf. No. **10**, p. 92).
		
		Morrow, *My Catholic Faith*, pp. 214–216 (cf. No. **24**, p. 92).

1. Be silent when someone says things to you or about you that you do not like — offer this to Jesus for poor people who do not know Him. 2. Each time you feel like doing wrong ask yourself: "Would Jesus do this?"	1. Read the poem, "Helping Others," No. **57**, p. 82. 2. Read and discuss story on kindness, No. **12**, Bk. 1, pp. 91–95. 3. Make a chart of things we can do to give good example to others.	Schumacher, *I Teach Catechism*, Vol. 1, pp. 177–182 (cf. No. **10**, p. 92). Morrow, *My Catholic Faith*, pp. 214–216 (cf. No. **24**, p. 92).

51

THINGS TO KNOW

	CONTENT	PUPIL TEXT	CHURCH YEAR	PRAYERS AND HYMNS
1st DAY	3. God's Sixth and Ninth Commandments: being pure and modest: *a)* in these laws God tells us to be pure in all our thoughts, desires, words, looks, and actions NOTE: Do not go too much into detail when teaching this commandment in order to safeguard the innocence of the child.	Lesson 15 Questions 87, 88, 89 Page 58		"Mother most pure, pray for us." Mental Prayer: 1. Picture Mary with beautiful lilies 2. Tell her how beautiful her pure soul is 3. Ask her to keep us pure, No. **48**.
2nd DAY	*b)* these laws forbid: 1) purposely thinking impure things 2) purposely speaking of impure things 3) purposely looking at impure things 4) purposely doing impure things; playing with my body or the bodies of others	Lesson 15 Question 90 Page 58		"St. Agnes, pray for us." "St. Aloysius, pray for us." "St. Maria Goretti, pray for us."
3rd DAY	4. God's Seventh and Tenth Commandments: respect for the property of others: *a)* in these laws God tells us: 1) to respect the property of others 2) to practice honesty in the use of all things 3) to be content with what is our own	Lesson 16 Questions 91, 92, 93 Page 61		Pray for those who are hungry and homeless that God may bless them.
4th DAY	*b)* these laws forbid: 1) stealing, cheating 2) helping others to steal 3) keeping things that do not belong to us 4) not returning valuable things that are found 5) not returning valuable things that are borrowed 6) breaking other people's things on purpose 7) wanting that which does not belong to us	Lesson 16 Question 94 Page 61		"Forgive us our trespasses as we forgive those who trespass against us."
5th DAY	Brief review, drill, and application to life of basic truths learned during this 19th week.			

50

THINGS TO DO

VIRTUES AND PRACTICES	SUGGESTED LEARNING ACTIVITIES	REFERENCES AND MATERIALS

Spiritual and Corporal Works of Mercy
 	
1. Keep pure and help others to be pure because your body is the temple of God:
  a) keep busy with work or play
  b) deny yourself something that you like to eat or do
  c) pray to our Blessed Mother
	1. Compare your bodies with a church and discuss why and how they must be kept pure.
	2. Observe pictures of Mary and Joseph with lilies and discuss the reason for the lilies.
	3. List the means for keeping pure:
	  a) sacraments and prayer, especially to Mary
	  b) keep ourselves busy
	  c) denying ourselves something we like
	  d) modesty in dress
		Schumacher, *I Teach Catechism*, Vol. 1, pp. 182–185 (cf. No. **10**, p. 92), Cat. 4, p. 29.
		
		Morrow, *My Catholic Faith*, p. 220 (cf. No. **24**, p. 92).

1. Keep away from the dangers to purity and help others to stay away also:
  a) bad movies and television shows
  b) dirty comics
  c) friends who do impure things or who talk and laugh about impure things
	1. Read and discuss simple stories about St. Agnes, Little Flower, St. Aloysius, and St. Mary Goretti.
	2. Discuss ways of avoiding the dangers to purity:
	  a) be careful of the kind of movies and television shows that we see
	  b) be careful of the kind of magazines that we read
	  c) be careful of the kind of people with whom we associate
		Morrow, *My Catholic Faith*, p. 220 (cf. No. **24**, p. 92).
		
		Schumacher, *I Teach Catechism*, Vol. 1, pp. 182–185 (cf. No. **10**, p. 92).

1. Be honest and generous with others because God has been so good to you:
  a) return things you borrow
  b) take good care of other people's lawns, books, etc.
  c) sacrifice your money, toys, etc.
  d) leave the better things for others
	1. Illustrate the kinds of property that may belong to children, mothers, fathers, church, school, etc.
	2. Read and discuss stories of saints who gave away their goods to the poor (St. Martin, St. Elizabeth).
	3. Collect pictures of people who are poor.
	4. Plan a Food or Clothes Drive for the poor.
		Morrow, *My Catholic Faith*, p. 224 (cf. No. **24**, p. 92).
		
		Schumacher, *I Teach Catechism*, Vol. 1, pp. 185–189 (cf. No. **10**, p. 92).

1. Help others to be honest:
  a) give them a good example
  b) show displeasure when your friends do something dishonest or ask you to help them to be dishonest
	1. Discuss problems concerning the actions of people and tell what an honest person would do in such a case, No. **12**, Bk. I, p. 87.
	2. List some ways in which we could share our goods with others.
		Morrow, *My Catholic Faith*, p. 224 (cf. No. **24**, p. 92).
		
		Schumacher, *I Teach Catechism*, Vol. 1, pp. 185–189 (cf. No. **10**, p. 92).

THINGS TO KNOW

	CONTENT	PUPIL TEXT	CHURCH YEAR	PRAYERS AND HYMNS
1st DAY	Purification of the Blessed Virgin Mary: Candlemas Day (Presentation of the Child Jesus in the Temple) 1. Mary's obedience to the law of Moses 2. Christ, the Light of the World		February 2 Presentation of the Child Jesus No. **16**	Mental Prayer: 1. Think about Mary going with Jesus and Joseph to the temple. 2. Give our hearts to Jesus through the hands of Mary. 3. All for Jesus through Mary.
2nd DAY	Feast of St. Blase: 1. Story of St. Blase 2. Why we pray to St. Blase		February 3 St. Blase	"St. Blase, keep me from diseases of the throat."

3rd DAY	5. God's Eighth Commandment: being truthful:
	
	a) in this law God tells us:
	  1) to tell the truth at all times
	  2) to think kindly of and speak kindly about others
		Lesson 17
		Questions 95, 96
		Page 63
				Mental Prayer:
				1. Picture Jesus curing the dumb man: see how happy he is.
				2. Thank Jesus for giving us the power to talk.
				3. Ask Him to help us to say our kind and true things. No. **47**

4th DAY	*b*) this law forbids:
	  1) telling lies
	  2) thinking and saying mean things about others
	  3) telling lies about others
	  4) keeping unkind thoughts about others in my mind
		Lesson 17
		Question 97
		Page 63
				Pray for the courage to tell the truth even when it is hard.

5th DAY	Brief review, drill, and application to life of basic truths learned during this 20th week.			

52

THINGS TO DO

VIRTUES AND PRACTICES	SUGGESTED LEARNING ACTIVITIES	REFERENCES AND MATERIALS
1. Thank God every day because He has given you the grace to know Jesus, the Light of the World. 2. Ask God to let the priests, Brothers, and Sisters who work in pagan lands bring men to know Him.	1. Compare the offering of the Child Jesus in the Temple to His heavenly Father with a religious vocation. 2. Read and discuss poem "Candles," No. **57**, p. 44.	Horan, *Bible Lessons*, p. 141 (cf. No. **3**, p. 92). Morrow, *My Catholic Faith*, p. 63 (cf. No. **24**, p. 92).
1. Do kind deeds for those who are sick. 2. Suffer patiently when you are sick because Jesus suffered patiently for you.	1. Get our throats blessed. 2. Practice little health habits to prevent the spread of diseases.	
1. Comfort people who suffer by saying kind and courteous things to them: *a*) greet them with a smile *b*) tell them something pleasant *c*) ask if you may do something for them	1. Tell stories of Jesus healing the dumb man and discuss the power we have to speak and how we should use it. 2. Plan ways in which we can help people who need help.	Schumacher, *I Teach Catechism*, Vol. 1, pp. 189–193 (cf. No. **10**, p. 92). Morrow, *My Catholic Faith*, p. 232 (cf. No. **24**, p. 92). Doanne, *A Small Child's Bible*, p. 112 (cf. No. **1**, p. 92).
1. Give your love to Jesus by saying only kind things about others and refusing to listen to unkind things. 2. Be brave enough to tell the truth even when you feel ashamed.	1. Discuss the part of the story of Fatima which shows how the children suffered rather than tell a lie. 2. Children find stories in library readers of children who told the truth and read them to the class.	Morrow, *My Catholic Faith*, p. 232 (cf. No. **24**, p. 92). Schumacher, *I Teach Catechism*, Vol. 1, pp. 189–193 (cf. No. **10**, p. 92).

THINGS TO KNOW

	CONTENT	PUPIL TEXT	CHURCH YEAR	PRAYERS AND HYMNS

1st DAY	6. Some laws of the Church:
	
	a) go to Mass on Sundays and holydays
	
	  1) holydays:
	    January 1 — Circumcision
	    May — Ascension Thursday
	    August 15 — Assumption of the Blessed Virgin Mary
	    November 1 — All Saints' Day
	    December 8 — Immaculate Conception
	    December 25 — Christmas Day
				Pray that many more people may belong to the Catholic Church.

2nd DAY	*b*) keep from eating meat on Fridays and other days appointed by the Church *c*) briefly recall the remaining commandments of the Church (NOTE: support of the Church should be emphasized.)	Lesson 18 Question 98 Page 65		"We adore Thee, O Christ, and bless Thee; because by Thy holy Cross Thou hast redeemed the world." (No. 191; 3 years.)
3rd DAY				
4th DAY				
5th DAY	Review, drill, and application to life of basic truths learned during this 21st week.			

THINGS TO DO

VIRTUES AND PRACTICES	SUGGESTED LEARNING ACTIVITIES	REFERENCES AND MATERIALS
1. Promise Jesus not to miss Mass on a holyday, even when it is hard for you to do so.	1. Make a chart of the holydays with a picture of each and the date of each. 2. Discuss why these laws were made by Holy Mother Church. 3. Illustrate the keeping of these commandments.	Brennan, *Angel Food*, p. 17 (cf. No. **12**, p. 92). Morrow, *My Catholic Faith*, p. 236 (cf. No. **24**, p. 92). Schumacher, *I Teach Catechism*, Vol. 2, p. 337 (cf. No. **10**, p. 92).
1. Comfort Jesus who suffered and died on a Friday: *a)* never eat meat on this day even when others do so *b)* make the Way of the Cross	1. Discuss why the Church made this law. 2. Tell stories of Catholics who keep this law even when others make fun of them.	Morrow, *My Catholic Faith*, p. 236 (cf. No. **24**, p. 92). Schumacher, *I Teach Catechism*, Vol. 2, p. 337 (cf. No. **10**, p. 92).

UNIT IV. *HOW GOD PARDONS SIN*

I. INTRODUCTION FOR THE TEACHER

This unit discusses the sacraments of Baptism and Penance. In considering the sacrament of Baptism, the teacher should emphasize its effects, since it is one which the children here already received. The discussions on the sacrament of Penance should be aimed at preparing the children for its worthy reception. The teacher should also strive to develop an attitude of appreciation and confidence in God's mercy and justice.

II. OBJECTIVES

A. To gain a clear understanding of the need of the sacrament of Baptism and an appreciation of its effects.

B. To learn the kinds of actual sin we commit and how to examine our conscience to find them.

C. To learn how Christ bestowed the power to forgive sin upon the Apostles and all priests and to appreciate its effects in our lives.

D. To attain the ability to prepare properly for confession and to make a good confession.

E. To develop a deep appreciation for and confidence in God's mercy as He extends it to us in the sacrament of Penance.

III. SUBJECT MATTER

A. How God in His mercy takes away Original Sin.

B. How God in His mercy takes away our own sins (actual sins).

C. What I must do to receive the sacrament of Penance worthily.

A SUGGESTED DEVELOPMENT LESSON PLAN

I. SUBJECT MATTER

A. General instruction on the seven sacraments (cf. p. 58, First Day).

II. TYPE

Development

III. OBJECTIVES

A. To acquaint the child with the names and the meaning of the seven sacraments in general.

B. To develop a deeper appreciation of God's love for us in giving us these helps to gain heaven.

C. To instill the desire to obtain the graces imparted by the sacraments.

IV. SUGGESTED PROCEDURE

A. Approach

Discuss the fact that when someone loves us very much he often shows his love by giving us a gift. Our Lord gave us a very big gift when He gave us the sacraments. Jesus saves us through the Church with the sacraments.

B. Presentation

1. What the sacraments are (outward sign):

    Our Lord loves us so very much that He wants each of us to live with Him in heaven forever and forever. Since He wants to make it easy for us to do so. He has given us the seven sacraments. (Draw a chasm, labeling it "Hell," across this place a ladder. Draw also the sacrament rope — explain how we must hold tightly to the rope in order to avoid sin.) *Chalk Talks* — Part II, p. 5.

    Each of the sacraments has a special sign to help us know it. Tell me what these signs mean: a gasoline pump; ear muffs, mittens and galoshes; an umbrella; smoke. We learn to know many things by signs, don't we? Signs can be things we see or hear. And that is one way we know the sacraments. Each one has an outward sign to tell us what it is. Now think of a baby being baptized and see if you can tell the outward sign (show picture). Remember it is something you can see or hear.

2. Where they come from (instituted by Christ):

    Now if this gift is going to help us to heaven, whom do you suppose made it? Yes, Christ Himself did. He made it especially for each one of us because He loves us so much. If He did not make it, it would not be His gift would it? We have a very grown-up word that means Christ made the sacraments. See if you can say it — "instituted." Now tell me what instituted means.

3. What they do (give grace):

    What do you think the sacraments might do for us? Yes, make us holy. They give us grace. Everyone needs grace to get into heaven. Grace makes us spiritually beautiful and our Lord wants us to be as beautiful as possible when we come to live with Him. In fact, as soon as you are beautiful with grace He comes and makes Himself at home in you. You have grace in you now because you were baptized. So just think, you have our Lord in you right now!

4. How many sacraments are there? Brief explanation of each.

5. Let's very quickly find out the names of the sacraments and what they do. Later on we'll study each one.

Baptism — washes away original sin.

Confirmation — makes us strong soldiers of Jesus Christ.

Holy Eucharist — is the Body and Blood of Jesus Christ under the form of bread and wine.

Penance — takes away the sins committed after Baptism.

The Anointing of the Sick — anointing the sick with holy oils to prepare them to die — takes away sin.

Holy Orders — the sacrament by which young men become priests.

Matrimony — the sacrament which unites a man and woman in marriage.

C. Organization

1. What wonderful gift did Jesus Christ give to us?
2. Why did He give us this gift?
3. If we use this gift all our lives where will we go?
4. What will this gift help us to avoid?
5. What do you mean by an outward sign?
6. Where did the sacraments come from?
7. What does "instituted" mean?
8. What do you receive each time you receive a sacrament?
9. How does God feel about a person who has grace?
10. What sacraments have you already received?
11. Do you know what it did for you?
12. Are you going to receive other sacraments this year?

D. Virtues and Practices

1. Make little sacrifices to obtain grace for ourselves and for others.
2. Compose little "Thank-You-Prayers" for this wonderful gift.
3. Talk to Jesus in our hearts and ask Him for more grace.

E. Assignment

Catechism Questions: 99, 100 at the end of Lesson 19.

V. SUGGESTED LEARNING ACTIVITIES

A. Discuss the meaning of the terms: *outward sign, instituted, grace.*

B. Start a class booklet on the sacraments. Correlate with English to compose a story about each sacrament.

C. Discussion and appreciation of the poem, "The Sacraments" (from *Verses for Tiny Tots*, B. J. Moran: The Bruce Publishing Co., Milwaukee, 1946).

VI. REFERENCES AND MATERIALS

A. Teacher's References.

1. Baierl, Rt. Rev. Joseph J., *The Sacraments and Prayer Explained*, St. Paul, Minn., Catechetical Guild Ed. Soc., Vol. II, p. 249 f.

2. Josita, Sister Mary, *Sing a Song of Holy Things*, Tower Press, Milwaukee.

3. O'Connor, Jerome F., S.J., Hayden, William, S.J., *Chalk Talks*, St. Louis, Mo., The Queen's Work, Part II, pp. 5–6.

4. Schumacher, Rt. Rev. Msgr., M.A., *I Teach Catechism*, New York, Benziger Bros., Inc., 1946, p. 188 f.

THINGS TO KNOW

	CONTENT	PUPIL TEXT	CHURCH YEAR	PRAYERS AND HYMNS

1st DAY	A. How God in His mercy takes away original sin.
	
	1. General instructions on the seven sacraments:
	  a) what they are
	  b) where they come from
	  c) how many sacraments are there?
	    1) brief explanation of each
		Lesson 19
		Questions 99, 100
		Pages 67–68
				Children compose original prayers as each sacrament is presented.

2nd DAY	*d*) what the sacraments do 1) brief explanation of "Grace"			1. Compose original prayers asking for God's grace.
3rd DAY	(Ash Wednesday) 1. Meaning of Lent 2. How we should keep Lent		The Lenten Season	Mental Prayer: 1. Picture Jesus in His sufferings. 2. Ask Him to help us bear our sufferings as He did, No. **48**, p. 20.

4th DAY	2. The sacrament of Baptism:
	  a) what it is
	  b) what it does:
	    1) takes away original sin
	    2) makes us children of God
	  c) why we need the sacrament of Baptism
	  d) renewal of the Baptism promises (NOTE: see Catechism Lesson 19.)
		Lesson 19
		Questions 101–104
		Page 68
				"O Jesus, I believe in You. O Jesus, I hope in You. O Jesus, I love You."
				
				"Glory be to the Father"
				
				"Sacred Heart of Jesus, Thy kingdom come" (No. 228; 300 days).

5th DAY	Brief review, drill, and application to life of the basic truths learned during this 22nd week.			

THINGS TO DO

VIRTUES AND PRACTICES	SUGGESTED LEARNING ACTIVITIES	REFERENCES AND MATERIALS
1. Make little sacrifices to obtain grace for yourself and for others.	1. Chalk Talk — Part II, p. 16 — the Seven Streams of Grace or the Road to Heaven. 2. Discuss pictures showing the various sacraments. 3. Illustrate a class booklet on the sacraments. 4. Read and discuss poem, "The Sacraments," No. **57**, p. 80.* 5. Suggested Filmstrip: The Sacraments in General (cf. No. **67**, Unit 11).*	Brennan, *Angel Food,* p. 26 (cf. No. **12**, p. 92).* Morrow, *My Catholic Faith,* p. 250 (cf. No. **24**, p. 92).*
1. Ask Mary to help you obtain as many graces as possible each day.	1. Illustrate the life of grace by drawing a picture of a bus with the trolley on the wire. 2. Discuss the meaning of the terms: sanctifying grace actual grace 3. Suggested Filmstrip: The Holy Spirit and Grace (cf. No. **67**, Unit 7).*	Morrow, *My Catholic Faith,* pp. 250–252 (cf. No. **24**, p. 92).* Schumacher, *I Teach Catechism,* Vol. 1, p. 215 (cf. No. **10**, p. 92).*
1. In order to console Jesus and to help Him to carry His cross, select a resolution to be kept during this season: *a*) abstaining *b*) attending Mass *c*) attending Lenten devotions	1. Discuss ways and means of making sacrifices during Lent. 2. Post pictures of the Stations of the Cross. 3. Discuss and compose original prayers. 4. Plan a device for the lenten practices. 5. Read poem, "Stations of the Cross," No. **57**, pp. 61–74.*	Morrow, *My Catholic Faith,* p. 241 (cf. No. **24**, p. 92).*
1. Pray for missionaries and for poor pagan children. 2. Offer sacrifices for the missions. 3. Be proud that you are a Catholic. 4. Show God you are grateful for belonging to a Catholic family. 5. Pray for members of your family who may not be Catholics.	1. Discuss the ceremony for a simple baptism: *a*) actions *b*) words 2. Let the children find out the date of their baptism. 3. Visit the baptismal font in Church. 4. Discuss the meaning and the formula for renewing the Baptismal Promises. 5. Read stories about missionaries administering the sacrament of Baptism (mission magazines).	Morrow, *My Catholic Faith,* pp. 252–257 (cf. No. **24**, p. 92).* Morrow, *My Catholic Faith,* pp. 252–257 (cf. No. **24**, p. 92).*

* For all keyed references in boldface type, see Teacher Bibliography, pp. 92–93, at end of this Teacher's Manual.

57

THINGS TO KNOW

	CONTENT	PUPIL TEXT	CHURCH YEAR	PRAYERS AND HYMNS

1st DAY	B. How God in His mercy takes away our own sins (actual sins).
	
	1. Sin is disobedience to God's laws:
	  a) sin offends God
	  b) story of Cain and Abel
		Lesson 20
		Questions 107–108
		Page 71
				"My God, I believe, I adore, I hope, and I love thee. I ask pardon for those who do not believe, nor adore, nor love you."

2nd DAY	2. Kinds of actual sin:
	  a) mortal sin:
	    1) what it is
	    2) what it does
		Lesson 20
		Questions 109, 110, 111
		Pages 71–72
				"Mother mine, deliver me from mortal sin."

3rd DAY	*b)* venial sin:
	    1) what it is
	    2) what it does
		Lesson 20
		Questions 114, 115
		Page 72
				"Mother of mercy, pray for us."
				(No. 304; 300 days.)

4th DAY	*c)* conditions necessary:
	    1) mortal sin
	    2) venial sin
		Lesson 20
		Questions 113, 116
		Page 72
				"My God, I love Thee."
				(No. 39; 300 days.)

5th DAY	Brief review, drill, and application to life of the basic truths learned during this 23rd week.			

60

THINGS TO DO

VIRTUES AND PRACTICES	SUGGESTED LEARNING ACTIVITIES	REFERENCES AND MATERIALS
1. Ask for the courage not to hurt God and to keep others from hurting Him by sin.	1. Read and discuss the story of Cain and Abel. 2. Discuss the difference between original sin and actual sin (Chart). 3. Suggested Filmstrip: Original and Actual Sin; Visualized First Communion Catechism, cf. No. **67**, A 924-4.	Morrow, *My Catholic Faith*, pp. 42–43 (cf. No. **24**, p. 92). Horan, *Bible Lessons*, p. 13 (cf. No. **3**, p. 92).
1. Ask for the grace never to commit a mortal sin.	1. List ways in which children might be guilty of mortal sin: *a*) missing Mass *b*) eating meat on Friday 2. Discuss reasons for reception of the sacrament of Penance after having committed mortal sin. 3. Read the story "A Piece of White Ribbon," No. **12**, Bk. 1, p. 23. 4. Read — discuss poems, "Sin," No. **57**, pp. 86, 87; "Pardon Me, Jesus."	Morrow, *My Catholic Faith*, pp. 44–45 (cf. No. **24**, p. 92). Schumacher, *I Teach Catechism*, Vol. 1, p. 66 (cf. No. **10**, p. 92).
1. Ask for the grace and the courage to keep away from venial sins because they too hurt God.	1. Children suggest possible venial sins. List them. 2. Discuss reasons why children do commit sin. 3. List ways in which boys and girls can lead others into sin.	Schumacher, *I Teach Catechism*, Vol. 1, pp. 68, 69 (cf. No. **10**, p. 92). Morrow, *My Catholic Faith*, pp. 46, 47 (cf. No. **24**, p. 92).
1. Never forget that God sees you at all times.	1. Teacher gives examples: Children tell whether it was a mortal sin, venial sin, or no sin. 2. Discuss the three things necessary for a mortal sin. 3. Read the story: "The Voice at the Window," No. **12**, Bk. 4, p. 7.	Schumacher, *I Teach Catechism*, Vol. 1, pp. 68–69 (cf. No. **10**, p. 92). Morrow, *My Catholic Faith*, pp. 46, 47 (cf. No. **24**, p. 92).

THINGS TO KNOW

	CONTENT	PUPIL TEXT	CHURCH YEAR	PRAYERS AND HYMNS
1st DAY	3. Jesus forgave the peoples' sins when they were sorry: *a*) story of Mary Magdalen *b*) story of the Good Thief			"Lord, remember me!"

2nd DAY	4. Jesus gave His power of forgiving sins to His Apostles and to all priests:
	
	a) institution of the sacrament of Penance:
	  1) what it is
	  2) what it does
		Lesson 21
		Question 117
		Page 75
				"My Jesus, Mercy."
				(No. 70; 300 days.)

3rd DAY	3) why we need it			Original prayers of thanksgiving to God for giving us the sacrament of Penance.
4th DAY	C. What I must do to receive the sacrament of Penance worthily. 1. Story of the Prodigal Son	Lesson 21 Question 121 Page 76		"O God, be merciful to me, the sinner" (No. 14; 500 days).
5th DAY	Brief review, drill, and application to life of the basic truths learned during this 24th week.			

THINGS TO DO

VIRTUES AND PRACTICES	SUGGESTED LEARNING ACTIVITIES	REFERENCES AND MATERIALS

1. Forgive others when they hurt you because Jesus forgives you when you sin.	1. Tell and discuss the story of Mary Magdalen or the Good Thief:
	
	  a) their wicked lives
	  b) their sorrow
	  c) the kindness of Jesus
	  d) their reward
	2. Discuss pictures of Mary Magdalen or the Good Thief.
	3. Discuss ways in which we can forgive others when they have offended us.
		Johnson, *The Bible Story*, p. 177 (cf. No. **4**, n. 92).
		
		Luke 23:39–43.

1. No matter how many sins you have committed or how big they are, always remember that they are forgiven when the priest gives you absolution.	1. Tell the story of Easter Sunday night. 2. Show that Penance is really a sacrament. (It has the three things necessary to make a sacrament.) 3. Discuss the words of absolution used by the priest in confession. 4. Suggested Filmstrip: Penance (cf. No. **67**, Unit 15).	Schumacher, *I Teach Catechism*, Vol. 1, p. 228 (cf. No. **10**, p. 92). Morrow, *My Catholic Faith*, pp. 300–301 (cf. No. **24**, p. 92).
1. Encourage others to receive the sacrament of Penance often.	1. Compare a soul in sin with a sick body. JESUS IS THE DOCTOR OF OUR SOULS.	Morrow, *My Catholic Faith*, p. 301 (cf. No. **24**, p. 92).

1. Make an effort to bring lax parents back to the sacraments.	1. Tell the story of the Prodigal Son.
	
	  a) he knew that he had done wrong
	  b) he was sorry for what he had done
	  c) he made up his mind not to sin again
	  d) he told his father that he had sinned
	  e) he wanted to make up for his sins
	2. Dramatize the story.
		Horan, *Bible Lessons*, p. 200 (cf. No. **3**, p. 92).
		
		Johnson, *The Bible Story*, p. 182 (cf. No. **4**, p. 92).
		
		Schumacher, *I Teach Catechism*, Vol. 1, p. 232 (cf. No. **10**, p. 92).
		
		Morrow, *My Catholic Faith*, p. 304 (cf. No. **24**, p. 92).

THINGS TO KNOW

	CONTENT	PUPIL TEXT	CHURCH YEAR	PRAYERS AND HYMNS
1st DAY	1. Before Confession pray to the Holy Ghost:			"Come, O Holy Spirit, help me to know all my sins. Help me to be very sorry for them. Help me to make up my mind to do them no more. Help me to tell them to the priest; help me to do my penance."
2nd DAY	*a*) I find out my sins			"O Mary, conceived without sin, pray for us who have recourse to thee." (No. 357; 300 days.)
3rd DAY	*b*) I am sorry for my sins: 1) sorrow for sin because of God's just punishment: (*a*) purgatory: a place of punishment to clean us of venial sins (*b*) hell: a place of everlasting suffering for those who die in mortal sin			"Mother of love, of sorrow and of mercy, pray for us." (No. 300; 300 days.)
4th DAY	2) sorrow for sin because of God's goodness to us: (*a*) creation (*b*) providence (*c*) redemption			Compose acts of perfect contrition.
5th DAY	Brief review, drill, and application to life of the basic truths learned during this 25th week.			

THINGS TO DO

VIRTUES AND PRACTICES	SUGGESTED LEARNING ACTIVITIES	REFERENCES AND MATERIALS
1. Ask the Holy Ghost to help you make a good Confession.	1. Discuss the need of light to find something that is in the dark. (The Holy Spirit is the light of our souls.) 2. Read and discuss the story: "Hello Halo," No. **45**.	
1. Examine your conscience before going to bed each night.	1. Aid the children to find out their sins by directing them to think about the things God told them to do in the Ten Commandments. 2. Begin a frieze or class booklet illustrating the five things necessary to make a good confession.	Schumacher, *I Teach Catechism*, Vol. 1, pp. 98–99 (cf. No. **10**, p. 92). Morrow, *My Catholic Faith*, pp. 302–303 (cf. No. **24**, p. 92).
1. Pray for the souls in purgatory.	1. Discuss how God punished the sin of the Bad Angels and of Adam and Eve. 2. God will also punish us when we sin. 3. Explain the terms: heartily — offend — detest. 4. Read the story: "The Most Beautiful Thing in the World," No. **12**, Bk. I, p. 35.	Morrow, *My Catholic Faith*, pp. 304–307 (cf. No. **24**, p. 92). *My Catholic Faith*, pp. 156–157, 164–165 (cf. No. **24**, p. 92).
1. Say an Act of Contrition before going to bed at night.	1. Recall stories of Creation — the Goodness of God — the Passion. 2. Collect and assemble pictures showing the goodness of God. Add these pictures to the frieze or booklet. 3. Explain the terms: All-good, deserving.	

THINGS TO KNOW

	CONTENT	PUPIL TEXT	CHURCH YEAR	PRAYERS AND HYMNS
1st DAY	(Feast of St. Patrick) (Feast of St. Joseph)		March 17 St. Patrick March 19 St. Joseph	"St. Patrick, pray for us." "St. Joseph, pray for us." "Jesus, Mary, and Joseph."
2nd DAY	*c*) I make up my mind not to sin again: 1) I pray for God's help. 2) I will not sin again.			Original prayers to ask God to keep me from sin.
3rd DAY	2. In the confessional: *a*) I go into the confessional and kneel *b*) I tell my sins to the priest *c*) suggested formula for the Confession of our sins: 1) I make the sign of the cross and say: "Bless me, Father, for I have sinned" (after first confession — "My last confession was .... weeks ago").	Lesson 21 Question 122 Page 76		"Jesus, help me to receive the sacrament of Penance worthily."
4th DAY	2) I tell my sins (begin with "I" and end with .... "times"). 3) I am sorry for these and all the sins of my past life especially for ..... 4) I listen to the talk the priest gives me. 5) I listen to the penance the priest gives me. 6) I say the Act of Contrition loud enough for the priest to hear. 7) I leave the confessional after the priest has said, "God bless you."			
5th DAY	Brief review, drill, and application to life of the basic truths learned during this 26th **week**.			

THINGS TO DO

VIRTUES AND PRACTICES	SUGGESTED LEARNING ACTIVITIES	REFERENCES AND MATERIALS
1. Obey God's laws so that by being good other people will learn from you how to love and serve God as they learned from St. Joseph and St. Patrick. 2. Ask for the grace of a Happy Death for yourself and for your family.	1. Tell the stories of the lives of St. Patrick and St. Joseph, No. **34**, p. 18, p. 16. 2. Discuss pictures of St. Patrick and St. Joseph. 3. Discuss ways of imitating the lives of these saints.	Butler, *Lives of the Saints* (cf. No. **29**, p. 92).
1. Correct one little fault today so that you will please God.	1. Draw the picture and add to the frieze or class booklet. 2. Explain the terms: "Firmly resolve," "near occasions." 3. Recite the entire Act of Contrition.	Morrow, *My Catholic Faith,* pp. 308–309 (cf. No. **24**, p. 92).
1. Be quiet and patient and prayerful while waiting your turn for Confession.	1. Take the children to church and let them see the confessional. NOTE: where the priest sits. Where we kneel (stand if too small). The grating and the slide. The Crucifix. 2. Show the children where to stand or kneel while waiting for their turn to go to confession. 3. Tell the children what to do while waiting — *pray, examine, be sorry, promise.* 4. Make a picture and add it to the frieze or class booklet.	Morrow, *My Catholic Faith,* pp. 310–313 (cf. No. **24**, p. 92).

THINGS TO KNOW

	CONTENT	PUPIL TEXT	CHURCH YEAR	PRAYERS AND HYMNS

1st DAY	3. After Confession:
	
	  a) I do or say the penance that the priest gives me:
	    1) when it is to be done
	    2) what should be done if the penance is forgotten
		Lesson 21
		Question 123
		Page 77
			March 25
			
			Feast of the Annunciation
				Original prayers for the priest who heard our confession.

2nd DAY	3) prayer of thanksgiving 4) prayer of petition to help us keep our promises			Compose original prayers of thanksgiving to God for taking away our sins.

3rd DAY	*b*) The Seal of Confession
	    1) how the priest keeps it a secret
	    2) how we must keep it a secret
		Lesson 21
		Question 124
		Page 77
				"O Jesus, help me always to love and make use of this Holy Sacrament."

4th DAY	Immediate Preparation for Confession			
5th DAY	Brief review, drill, and application to life of the basic truths learned during this 27th week.			

THINGS TO DO

VIRTUES AND PRACTICES	SUGGESTED LEARNING ACTIVITIES	REFERENCES AND MATERIALS
1. Do extra little penances to make up for sins you have committed.	1. Make a visit to the church to show the children where to go and what to do after leaving the Confessional. 2. Draw the picture and add it to the frieze or class booklet.	Morrow, *My Catholic Faith*, p. 314 (cf. No. **24**, p. 92). Schumacher, *I Teach Catechism*, Vol. 1, p. 102 (cf. No. **10**, p. 92).
1. Ask for the grace to be strong enough to say "no" to temptation.	1. Discuss ways and means of avoiding sin in the future. Make a class chart.	
1. Pray each day for the grace of a good Confession for all the children in your class.	1. Tell the story of St. John Nepomucene. 2. Discuss the importance of the secrecy of confession, No. **51**, p. 336.	Morrow, *My Catholic Faith*, p. 316 (cf. No. **24**, p. 92).
	1. Allow each child to recite the Prayer to the Holy Spirit, the formula for confession, and the Act of Contrition. 2. Title, label, and discuss picture in the class booklet as review preparatory to the reception of the sacrament of Penance.	

UNIT V. *HOW GOD CARES FOR OUR SOULS THROUGH THE HOLY EUCHARIST*

I. INTRODUCTION FOR THE TEACHER

The understanding of the basic truths about the Holy Eucharist which are developed in this unit enable the child to acquire the knowledge and love necessary to receive his Eucharistic God worthily and with deep devotion.

II. OBJECTIVES

A. To appreciate how our Lord, by giving us the Mass and the Holy Eucharist, showed His solicitude for the natural life of man but especially for his supernatural life.

B. To establish an attitude of gratitude for these gifts.

C. To inspire the children with a desire and a sincere longing to make use of these gifts.

D. To acquire the knowledge of how to prepare well for First Holy Communion.

E. To instill the desire to want to make a return for these gifts by a love for Holy Mass and the frequent reception of the Holy Eucharist.

III. SUBJECT MATTER

Passion Sunday to Easter Sunday (Teacher handles at appropriate time.)

A. Jesus promises to give us food for our supernatural life.

B. Jesus keeps His promise.

C. The Mass: We offer Jesus to God, His heavenly Father.

D. Holy Communion: The Food of our souls.

A SUGGESTED DEVELOPMENT LESSON PLAN

I. SUBJECT MATTER

A. Jesus Keeps His Promise (p. 74, No. B)

II. TYPE

Development

III. OBJECTIVES

A. To realize how Jesus, by giving us the sacrament of Holy Eucharist, showed us how deeply concerned He is with our supernatural life.

B. To establish an attitude of gratitude for this great gift.

C. To develop a desire to make use of this great gift.

IV. SUGGESTED PROCEDURE

A. Approach

Jesus often showed His love and kindness to people when He lived here on earth. We know this by the many miracles that He worked. On Monday we learned that Jesus showed His great power by performing the miracle of the Loaves and Fishes. We know that in performing this miracle Jesus promised a new bread, the Bread of Life, the Bread that came down from heaven.

B. Presentation

1. The First Mass — The Institution of the Holy Eucharist

   a) The Last Supper

   On the first Holy Thursday, Jesus celebrated the feast of the Pasch with His Apostles. This feast had to be prepared in a very special way — according to the Law of Moses. They had roast lamb, bread made without yeast, lettuce, and wine. When Jesus and the twelve Apostles sat down to supper, they did everything that the Law of Moses commanded. They said prayers, sang hymns, and Jesus told the story of the First Pasch — the story of Moses leading the Jewish people out of the slavery of Egypt. Jesus ate supper with His Apostles for the last time. The next day Jesus would die on the cross.

   b) The words used by Jesus to change Bread and Wine into His own Body and Blood.

   After the Paschal Supper was over, Jesus took bread, blessed it, broke and gave it to the Apostles saying, "Take and eat; this is My body." Then Jesus took the cup of wine and said, "All of you drink of this; for this is My blood of the new covenant which is being shed for many unto the forgiveness of sins." Do this in remembrance of Me." By these words, Jesus instituted the sacrament of the Holy Eucharist. Jesus could do this because He is God and God can do all things. This was the First Mass. The Apostles received their First Holy Communion.

   c) The meaning of this Sacrament

   Jesus told the Apostles, and through them all His priests, to do as He did. The priest does this every day at the Consecration of the Mass. When the priest changes bread and wine it becomes the living Body, Blood, Soul, and Divinity of Jesus Christ. The Sacred Host looks like a round piece of bread. It tastes like bread but It is not bread. The Sacred Host is really Jesus. The same Jesus who was born on Christmas Day. The same Jesus who died on the cross on Good Friday.

At the Communion of the Mass people receive Jesus in the Holy Eucharist. Jesus will give Himself to you for the first time on your First Communion Day.

C. Organization

1. When did Jesus institute the sacrament of the Holy Eucharist?
2. What is the sacrament of the Holy Eucharist?
3. What did Jesus do at the Last Supper?
4. How could Jesus change bread and wine into His Body and Blood?
5. Who were with Jesus at the Last Supper?

D. Virtues and Practices

1. I will show my appreciation for this Great Gift of Jesus in the Holy Eucharist by greater reverence and attention at Holy Mass, especially during the Consecration of the Mass.

2. Jesus kept His Promise when He gave Himself in the Holy Eucharist. I will be faithful in keeping promises that I make to others.

E. Assignment

Catechism question 125 at the end of Lesson 22.

F. Prayers and Hymns

1. Make an original prayer thanking Jesus for the Gift of the Holy Eucharist.
2. Ask Jesus to help you prepare yourself for receiving this Great Gift for the first time.

V. SUGGESTED LEARNING ACTIVITIES

1. Show and discuss a picture illustrating the institution of the Holy Eucharist at the Last Supper.
2. Explain terms — "institution" — "Holy Eucharist" — "Sacred Host."
3. Tell the story of the Last Supper to others.

VI. REFERENCES AND MATERIALS

A. Teacher
   1. Johnson, *The Bible Stories*, p. 201.
   2. Horan, *Bible Lessons*, p. 213.

B. Pupil
   1. *Jesus Comes*, Lesson 22.

THINGS TO KNOW

	CONTENT	PUPIL TEXT	CHURCH YEAR	PRAYERS AND HYMNS

1st DAY	(Passion Sunday)
	
	1. The meaning of Passion Sunday
	2. Signs of sorrow:
	  a) covering of the crucifix
	  b) covering of the statues
				Original prayers in honor of our suffering Saviour.

2nd DAY	(Palm Sunday)
	
	1. How the people of Jerusalem honored Jesus on this day
	2. How the Church celebrates this day
	3. Significance of blessed palm:
	  a) how we use it
	  b) what it does for us
				"Hosanna to the Son of David."
				
				"Sacred Heart of Jesus, Thy kingdom come."
				(No. 228; 300 days.)

3rd DAY	(Holy Thursday)
	
	1. Story of the Last Supper
	2. How the Church celebrates this day
	3. Special ceremonies used in the Church:
	  a) the Mass
	  b) the Procession
	  c) the Repository
				"O Sacrament most holy, O sacrament divine! All praise and all thanksgiving, be every moment Thine."
				(No. 136; 300 days.)

4th DAY	(Good Friday) 1. Story of the First Good Friday 2. How the Church celebrates this day 3. Special ceremonies used in the Church			"We adore thee, O Christ and we bless Thee; because by Thy holy Cross Thou hast redeemed the world." (No. 191; 3 years.)
5th DAY	(Easter Sunday) 1. How Jesus showed that He was God 2. How the Church celebrates this day			"Alleluia! Alleluia!" Original prayers of adoration and of praise to our Risen Lord.

THINGS TO DO

VIRTUES AND PRACTICES	SUGGESTED LEARNING ACTIVITIES	REFERENCES AND MATERIALS
1. Make a special sacrifice to give up something you like very much for the love of Jesus.	1. Discuss the gospel story for Passion Sunday, John 8:59. 2. Look for some signs of sorrow in the Church. 3. Discuss the meaning of the word "passion." 4. Make a picture booklet of the events of the Passion.	Schumacher, *I Teach Catechism*, Vol. 2, p. 458 (cf. No. **10**, p. 92).* *My Daily Missal*
1. Be reverent in handling blessed palms. 2. Take some blessed palm for someone who is unable to come to church.	1. Discuss ways of praising God in church, in school, at home. 2. Discuss the use of blessed palms. 3. Compose a class "Holy Week Book." Make the page for Palm Sunday.	Johnson, *The Bible Story*, p. 198 (cf. No. **4**, p. 92).* *Daily Missal* Horan, *Bible Lessons*, p. 211 (cf. No. **3**, p. 92).*
1. Visit the Repository and thank Jesus for staying in the Blessed Sacrament. 2. Encourage others to make visits and attend "Holy Week" devotions. 3. Practice reverence in the presence of the Blessed Sacrament.	1. Discuss the meaning of the Repository, No. **12**, Bk. 1, pp. 49, 53, 57.* 2. Discuss why we kneel on two knees. 3. Continue work on the "Holy Week Book." Make the picture page for Holy Thursday. 4. Teach a hymn in honor of the Blessed Sacrament.	Morrow, *My Catholic Faith*, p. 371 (cf. No. **24**, p. 92).* Johnson, *The Bible Story*, p. 201 (cf. No. **4**, p. 92).* Horan, *Bible Lessons*, p. 212 (cf. No. **3**, p. 92).*
1. Use opportunities for making little sacrifices in union with the sacrifice of Christ on the cross. 2. Attend the devotions and venerate the crucifix.	1. Tell the story of the Passion and Death of Jesus. 2. Read and discuss the poem, "Jesus dies on the Cross," No. **57**, p. 72.* 3. List ways in which we can show honor to the Crucifix. 4. Continue work on the "Holy Week Book." Make the page for Good Friday.	Morrow, *My Catholic Faith*, p. 68 (cf. No. **24**, p. 92).* Horan, *Bible Lessons*, p. 218 (cf. No. **3**, p. 92).* Johnson, *The Bible Story*, p. 205 (cf. No. **4**, p. 92).*
1. Spread a spirit of joy and cheerfulness by doing many little kind acts for others.	1. Tell the story of the Resurrection of our Saviour. 2. Make a picture book of some of the events following the Resurrection. 3. Make the picture page for Easter Sunday for the "Holy Week Book."	Morrow, *My Catholic Faith*, pp. 70–71 (cf. No. **24**, p. 92).* Morrow, *My Catholic Faith*, pp. 72–73 (cf. No. **24**, p. 92).* Johnson, *The Bible Story*, p. 220 (cf. No. **4**, p. 92).* Horan, *Bible Lessons*, p. 227 (cf. No. **3**, p. 92).*

* For all keyed references in boldface type, see Teacher Bibliography, pp. 92–93, at end of this Teacher's Manual.

THINGS TO KNOW

	CONTENT	PUPIL TEXT	CHURCH YEAR	PRAYERS AND HYMNS

1st DAY	A. Jesus promises to give us food for our supernatural life.
	
	1. The miraculous multiplication of the loaves and fishes:
	  a) Jesus showed His love and kindness
	  b) Jesus showed His great power
				Give us this day our daily bread (Our Father).

2nd DAY	2. The promise of the Holy Eucharist:
	
	  a) Jesus promised a new bread
	  b) Jesus, the Bread of Life
				Original prayers in which we ask Jesus for the Bread of Life.
				
				"Jesus, Jesus, come to me."

3rd DAY	B. Jesus keeps His promise.
	
	1. The first Mass — the institution of the Holy Eucharist:
	  a) the Last Supper
	  b) the words used by Jesus to change bread and wine into His Body and Blood
	  c) the meaning of this Sacrament
		Lesson 22
		Question 125
		Page 80
				Original prayers of appreciation and of gratitude for the gift of the Holy Eucharist.

4th DAY	2. The Apostles receive their First Holy Communion.
	3. Jesus makes the Apostles His first priests:
	  a) Jesus gave the Apostles power to change bread and wine into His Body and Blood
	  b) all priests have this power
	  c) they use this power at Holy Mass
		Lesson 22
		Questions 126, 130
		Pages 80, 81
				1. Pray for priests so that Christ's work will continue.
				2. Say a special prayer for our priests and our bishops today.

5th DAY	4. Why Jesus gave us the Eucharist:
	
	  a) to help us love God — in the Mass we offer Him to God
	  b) to come to us in Holy Communion — He is the Food of our soul
	  c) to remain with us in the Blessed Sacrament — He is our Friend in the Tabernacle
				"Eternal Father, I offer Thee Thy Love. Come, sweet Jesus. Come, Jesus, in the Blessed Sacrament, I adore You."

THINGS TO DO

VIRTUES AND PRACTICES	SUGGESTED LEARNING ACTIVITIES	REFERENCES AND MATERIALS
1. Turn to God in prayer in all your needs. 2. Today, try to help someone who is poor.	1. Tell the story of the Multiplication of the Loaves and Fishes (John 6:1–15). 2. Discuss pictures that illustrate this particular miracle. 3. Dramatize this story. 4. Read and discuss the poem: "The Multiplication of the Loaves and Fishes" (cf. No. **60**, p. 67).	Johnson, *The Bible Story*, p. 186 (cf. No. **4**, p. 92).
1. Make some special sacrifice and pray today for "fallen-away Catholics" to come back to the Sacraments.	1. List ways in which we can help others to know Jesus in the Blessed Sacrament. 2. Dramatize the incident of Peter's profession of Faith. 3. Discuss the words, "Jesus, the Bread of Life." 4. Suggested Filmstrip: The Holy Eucharist (cf. No. **67**, Unit 13).	*Holy Bible*, John 6:22–59.
1. Show appreciation for the gift of the Holy Eucharist by great reverence and attention at Holy Mass. 2. Be faithful in keeping promises that you make.	1. Discuss pictures illustrating the institution of the Holy Eucharist. 2. Discuss the words of "Institution." 3. Discuss the meaning of the "Holy Eucharist." 4. Plan to tell the story of the Last Supper to some younger children.	Horan, *Bible Lessons*, p. 213 (cf. No. **3**, p. 92). Johnson, *The Bible Story*, p. 201 (cf. No. **4**, p. 92). Morrow, *My Catholic Faith*, pp. 269–270 (cf. No. **24**, p. 92).

1. Show great respect and reverence toward all priests at all times:
  a) cheerfully greet them
  b) offer to help them
  c) always be obedient to them
	1. Tell the story of how Jesus made the Apostles the first priests and gave them power to offer Holy Mass.
	2. Memorize the words that Jesus used to make the Apostles priests.
		Schumacher, *I Teach Catechism*, p. 245 (cf. No. **10**, p. 92).
		
		Morrow, *My Catholic Faith*, p. 262 (cf. No. **24**, p. 92).

1. Show your love for Jesus in the Blessed Sacrament by making visits to Jesus in the tabernacle today.	1. Make class charts listing ways in which we can honor Jesus Christ in the Mass, in Holy Communion; and in the Tabernacle. 2. Read and discuss the poem, "The Gold Cup," No. **57**, p. 89.	Morrow, *My Catholic Faith*, pp. 260–269 (cf. No. **24**, p. 92).

THINGS TO KNOW

	CONTENT	PUPIL TEXT	CHURCH YEAR	PRAYERS AND HYMNS
1st DAY	C. The Mass: We offer Jesus to God His heavenly Father. 1. What the Mass is: *a)* Christ offered Himself at the Last Supper *b)* Christ offered Himself on the cross *c)* Christ offers Himself in every Holy Mass	Lesson 23 Questions 132–136 Pages 86–87		"Eternal Father, I offer Thee Thy Son."
2nd DAY	2. What we do at Mass: The three principal parts: *a)* the Offertory: 1) the priest offers gifts to God — bread and wine 2) we offer gifts to God: ourselves, our prayers, our good deeds			"O God, I offer Thee this day, all I think, and do and say; uniting it with what was done on earth, by Jesus Christ, Thy Son."
3rd DAY	*b)* The Consecration and the Elevation: 1) what the priest does: (a) the priest changes bread into the Body of Jesus with the words, "This is My Body" (b) the priest changes wine into the Blood of Jesus with the words, "This is My Blood" (c) Jesus is present in every part of the consecrated Host; He is present in every part of the consecrated wine	Lesson 23 Questions 137–138 Page 87		"Jesus, my God, I adore Thee, here present in the Sacrament of Thy Love."
4th DAY	2) what we do: (a) we look at the Sacred Host and say, "My Lord and my God" (b) we look at the chalice and say, "My Lord and my God" 3) what Jesus does: (a) Jesus offers Himself to His heavenly Father (b) we offer Jesus to His heavenly Father through the priest			"My Lord and my God" (No. 133; 7 years).
5th DAY	*c)* The communion: 1) what the priest does: (a) the priest receives Jesus in his heart (b) the priest gives Jesus in Holy Communion to the people 2) what should we do: (a) we should receive Jesus in Holy Communion (b) we should make a spiritual communion when we are not able to receive sacramentally			Spiritual Communion (Original) (Cf. No. 164; 3 years.)

THINGS TO DO

VIRTUES AND PRACTICES	SUGGESTED LEARNING ACTIVITIES	REFERENCES AND MATERIALS
1. Show your love for your heavenly Father by attending the Mass on days when you are not obliged to do so. 2. Be thoughtful of others who have come to assist at Mass.	1. Make a class chart of the things that we can do to show that we really love the Mass. 2. Read and discuss the story, "Jesus' Workshop" or "The Priest of Times Square" (No. **12**, Bk. IV, pp. 68–71). 3. Read and discuss the poem, "My Visits" (No. **57**, p. 4). 4. Suggested Filmstrip: The Mass (cf. No. **67**, Unit 14).	Morrow, *My Catholic Faith*, pp. 270–271 (cf. No. **24**, p. 92).
1. Every time you offer Mass, Jesus offers Himself for you. Remember the Mass is the best gift you can give to God.	1. Read and discuss the story of the Last Supper. 2. Make a list of gifts that we can offer to God. 3. Begin a frieze or a class booklet illustrating the three principal parts of the Mass.	Morrow, *My Catholic Faith*, p. 288 (cf. No. **24**, p. 92). Schumacher, *I Teach Catechism*, Vol. 1, p. 76 (cf. No. **10**, p. 92).
1. Always listen to the warning bell that tells you Jesus is coming in the Mass and look up at the altar. 2. Try to help others know the true meaning of the Mass.	1. Discuss the central Act of the Mass: The Consecration and its holy meaning. 2. Show the relationship of words used by our Lord at the Last Supper and the Words of Consecration in the Mass used by the priest. 3. Study selected pictures which illustrate the Consecration and the Elevation.	Morrow, *My Catholic Faith*, p. 290 (cf. No. **24**, p. 92). Schumacher, *I Teach Catechism*, Vol. 2, p. 257 (cf. No. **10**, p. 92).
1. Always show special reverence at the Consecration and the Elevation and remember to say the indulgenced prayer, "My Lord and my God."	1. Discuss the meaning of the two sentences — "We offer Jesus to His heavenly Father through the priest," "Jesus offers Himself to His heavenly Father." 2. Continue Mass booklet or frieze and make the page illustrating the Consecration and Elevation.	Goebel, *Living by God's Law*, p. 143 (cf. Cat. 2, p. 98).
1. Try to make a Spiritual Communion not only at Mass — but often throughout the day and encourage others to do so.	1. Study selected pictures of the Mass — Offertory, Consecration, and Elevation and Communion and discuss the action of each. 2. Read and discuss stories of saints who showed special love for the Mass and desire for Holy Communion. 3. Continue the mass booklet or frieze and make a page illustrating the Communion of the Mass.	Morrow, *My Catholic Faith*, p. 291 (cf. No. **24**, p. 92). Schumacher, *I Teach Catechism*, Vol. 2, p. 258 (cf. No. **10**, p. 92).

THINGS TO KNOW

	CONTENT	PUPIL TEXT	CHURCH YEAR	PRAYERS AND HYMNS
1st DAY	D. Holy Communion: The food of our souls 1. How to prepare for Jesus' first visit: remote preparation: *a*) by prayer: Acts of Faith, Love, and Desire *b*) by making little sacrifices *c*) by visiting Jesus in the Blessed Sacrament *d*) by keeping free from sin *e*) by being obedient, kind, truthful, etc. *f*) by imitating other first communicants	Lesson 24 Question 139 Page 89		"Come, O Jesus, come."

2nd DAY	2. Holy Communion: What it means to me:
	
	a) who comes to me in Holy Communion:
	  1) the Sacred Host is Jesus; Jesus is God
	  2) the Sacred Host looks and tastes like bread
		Lesson 24
		Question 140
		Page 90
				"Jesus, I believe that You are really present in the Sacred Host."

3rd DAY	*b*) who Jesus is (approachableness of Jesus):
	
	  1) Jesus the friend of little children
	  2) stories that exemplify this love: tell a story each day during the preparatory period:
	    (a) Blessed Imelda — *Mine* magazine (Two), May, 1954
	    (b) St. Tarcisius — *This Is Our Town* (Third Reader), pp. 297–304
	    (c) Little Nellie — "True stories for First Communicants, *Jr. Cath. Mess.*, May, 1953, p. 8
	    (d) St. Gerard — *Mine* magazine (Three), April, 1949
	    (e) Pius X — *Mine* magazine (Two), June, 1954
				"St. Tarcisius, keep safe the children who are making their first Communion."

4th DAY	*c*) what Jesus does for me in Holy Communion:
	
	  1) Jesus lives in me and gives me grace to live a holy life
	  2) He strengthens me against temptation
				Original prayer —
				"Jesus, I want You.
				
				Jesus, I need You.
				
				Come, sweet Jesus, come.

5th DAY	*d*) why I want to receive Jesus:
	
	  1) good motives
	  2) unworthy motives
				Come, O come, sweet Jesus,
				Come to me and stay;
				For I want You, Jesus,
				More than I can say."

THINGS TO DO

VIRTUES AND PRACTICES	SUGGESTED LEARNING ACTIVITIES	REFERENCES AND MATERIALS
1. Make acts of self-denial in preparation for the coming of Jesus.	1. Compose class charts suggesting ways we can prepare for Jesus' first visit. 2. Learn prayers that must be memorized for First Communion day.	Morrow, *My Catholic Faith*, pp. 294–298 (cf. No. **10**, p. 92). Schumacher, *I Teach Catechism*, Vol. 1, pp. 246–247 (cf. No. **10**, p. 92).
1. Make acts of faith and trust in Jesus who has given Himself to you to be your spiritual food.	1. Discuss the difference between a consecrated Host and an unconsecrated Host. 2. Children copy a selection from a First Communion prayer and on it stencil in chalk a pattern of a chalice and host.	Morrow, *My Catholic Faith*, pp. 294–298 (cf. No. **24**, p. 92). Schumacher, *I Teach Catechism*, Vol. 1, pp. 247–249 (cf. No. **10**, p. 92).

1. Try to imitate other first communicants in their love and devotion to Jesus in the Holy Eucharist.	1. Read and discuss stories of first communicants:
	  a) let the children give their own comments on the moral of the stories
	  b) dramatize incidents from these stories
		Morrow, *My Catholic Faith*, pp. 294–298 (cf. No. **24**, p. 92).
		
		Schumacher, *I Teach Catechism*, Vol. 1, pp. 253–254 (cf. No. **10**, p. 92).

1. Keep your heart pure so that it will be a fitting "tabernacle" for Jesus. 2. Practice courage in opposing those who try to lead you into sin.	1. Discuss the meaning of Jesus' sacramental presence within us after Holy Communion. 2. Help the class draw up a list of ways showing how we can oppose those who might try to lead us into sin. 3. Read and discuss the story, "A King in Disguise," Bk. 12, No. **1**, p. 45. 4. Read and discuss poem, "Little Imelda," No. **57**, p. 94.	Schumacher, *I Teach Catechism*, Vol. 1, pp. 253–254 (cf. No. **10**, p. 92). Morrow, *My Catholic Faith*, pp. 294–298 (cf. No. **24**, p. 92).
1. Always receive Holy Communion to please Jesus and to become like Him.	1. Compare worthy motives with unworthy motives for the reception of Holy Communion. 2. Dramatize incidents which illustrate this. 3. Read and discuss the poem, "First Communion," No. **62**, p. 36.	Morrow, *My Catholic Faith*, pp. 294–298 (cf. No. **24**, p. 92).

THINGS TO KNOW

	CONTENT	PUPIL TEXT	CHURCH YEAR	PRAYERS AND HYMNS

1st DAY	3. What I must do to receive Holy Communion:
	  a) prepare my soul:
	    1) be free from mortal sin
	    2) say prayers before Holy Communion
		Lesson 24
		Question 141
		Page 90
				Prayers before Holy Communion
				
				Pupil Text — Page 7

2nd DAY	*b*) prepare my body:
	    1) by fasting — 1 hour, solid food and liquids except water
	    2) be neat and clean
		Lesson 24
		Question 142
		Page 90
				"Take my body, Jesus, eyes, and ears and tongue. Never let them, Jesus, help to do Thee wrong. Take my heart and fill it full of love for Thee. All I have I give Thee. Give Thyself to me."

3rd DAY	*c*) at the altar:
	    put head back slightly; open mouth moderately, wet the tongue; extend the tongue out a bit and rest it on the lower lip; draw the tongue back carefully; close the mouth; if the host sticks to the roof of the mouth use the tongue to get it down; swallow the Sacred Host as soon as possible being careful never to touch it
	  d) return to your place with hands folded, eyes looking down and begin prayers of thanksgiving immediately
		Lesson 24
		Question 143
		Page 90
				"Jesus, make me worthy to receive You."

4th DAY	4. **What I** should do after Holy Communion:
	  a) I talk with Jesus:
	    1) I tell Jesus that I believe He is in my heart (Faith)
	    2) I tell Jesus how much I love Him (Adoration)
	    3) I thank Jesus for coming to me (Thanksgiving)
	    4) I tell Jesus that I am sorry for all my sins (Contrition)
	    5) I ask Jesus to help me and others (Petition)
	    6) I promise Jesus to be good (Resolution)
				Page 8
				
				Prayers after Holy Communion

5th DAY	5. First Communion Day:
	  a) at home:
	    1) I think of Jesus and make the sign of the cross when I wake up
	    2) I say my morning prayers
	    3) I keep the fast
				Mental Prayer:
				1. Make a mental picture of Jesus who is coming into my heart.
				2. Ask Jesus and Mary to help me to get ready for Holy Communion.

THINGS TO DO

VIRTUES AND PRACTICES	SUGGESTED LEARNING ACTIVITIES	REFERENCES AND MATERIALS
1. Each day of your life ask God to keep you from mortal sin. 2. Do what you can to keep others from offending God.	1. Review and discuss the meaning of the three things necessary to make a sin mortal. 2. Continue to practice the prayers for Holy Communion. 3. Suggested Filmstrip: Preparation for Confession and Holy Communion (cf. No. **67**, A, 924-6).	Morrow, *My Catholic Faith*, pp. 296–297 (cf. No. **24**, p. 92).
1. Watch over yourself carefully so that you do not break your Communion Fast.	1. Read and discuss the story, "Joseph and Nicodemus," No. **12**, Bk. IV, p. 57.	
1. Ask God's help to make a special effort today to keep your heart pure in preparation for His coming.	1. Read and discuss the poem, "A Throne for My King," No. **57**, p. 92. 2. Study pictures of people receiving Holy Communion. 3. Write a letter to Jesus to tell Him how much we want Him to come to us in Holy Communion.	
1. Ask God to help you know how you can win others for Jesus. 2. Pray every day for children who have never received Jesus.	1. Read and discuss the poem, "After Holy Communion," No. **57**, p. 97. 2. Talk over and discuss the prayers of Thanksgiving from the children's prayer books.	Schumacher, *I Teach Catechism*, Vol. 1, p. 110 (cf. No. **10**, p. 92). Morrow, *My Catholic Faith*, p. 298 (cf. No. **24**, p. 92).
1. Think often today about all that Jesus has done for you. 2. Thank Jesus this day for having given Himself to you in Holy Communion.	1. Encourage frequent reception of Holy Communion. 2. Read and discuss the story, "The Golden Key," No. **12**, Bk. IV, p. 60.	Schumacher, *I Teach Catechism*, Vol. 1, pp. 108–109 (cf. No. **10**, p. 92).

THINGS TO KNOW

	CONTENT	PUPIL TEXT	CHURCH YEAR	PRAYERS AND HYMNS
1st DAY	b) on the way to church: 1) I say prayers to Jesus 2) I think of stories about Jesus			Prayers before Holy Communion Original prayers of love and desire Prayers after Holy Communion
2nd DAY	c) in church: 1) I pray 2) I listen to the sermon 3) I receive Holy Communion with love 4) I say prayers of thanksgiving			
3rd DAY	Subject to local customs: Renewal of Baptismal Vows (sometimes made at the conclusion of the study of the sacrament of Baptism) Enrollment in the Scapular			
4th DAY				
5th DAY				

THINGS TO DO

VIRTUES AND PRACTICES	SUGGESTED LEARNING ACTIVITIES	REFERENCES AND MATERIALS
Practice silence and recollection in preparation for Jesus' coming.		

UNIT VI. *HOW WE CAN SHOW OUR LOVE FOR GOD: THE PRACTICE OF RELIGION*

I. INTRODUCTION FOR THE TEACHER

This last unit is an over-all review of the preceding five units. Its purpose is to encourage the child to practice virtue thus enabling him to live the "Christ Life" through the imitation of Christ.

II. OBJECTIVES

A. To establish an understanding of the obligation to attend Holy Mass and to receive the sacraments during the summer vacation period.
B. To develop a knowledge and an appreciation of the important role Mary should play in our daily lives.
C. To show our love and gratitude to God in our daily life through prayer and devotional practices.

III. SUBJECT MATTER

A. The Practice of Religion: Prayer and Devotional Practices
B. Obedience to God's Laws in Imitation of Our Blessed Mother
C. Faithful Attendance at Holy Mass
D. Frequent Reception of the Sacraments of Penance and Holy Eucharist

A SUGGESTED DEVELOPMENT LESSON PLAN

I. SUBJECT MATTER
Prayers and devotional practices (cf. p. 86, First Day)

II. TYPE
Development

III. OBJECTIVES
A. To show our love and gratitude to God in our daily lives through prayer and devotional practices

IV. SUGGESTED PROCEDURE

A. Approach
In the past few months we have learned many things about God, His Blessed Mother, and the saints. Today we are going to talk about the things we can do to show God that we really love Him and are thankful for all the gifts that He has given us.

B. Presentation
1. Prayer and Devotional Practices

What would happen if you and your best friend would stop seeing each other? Suppose you never called him up or wrote to him? Don't you think that after a little while you would be like strangers?

Jesus is our best Friend, yet sometimes we treat Him like a stranger. While we are here at school it is very easy to visit Jesus. We often go into the church to talk to Jesus. We think of Him often during the day, say many little prayers, and think about Jesus right here in the classroom.

But, what happens in the summertime when we are not at school? Does Jesus stop loving and caring for us in the vacation time? No, Jesus loves us and watches over us at all times.

Let us not forget to say our prayers, to visit Jesus and to think about Him often during the summer vacation. What prayers do you think we should say? Discuss. List on a chart.

Today we are going to print a sign for ourselves that will help us remember to say our prayers during the vacation time. We ought to put this sign in our bedroom so we can see it often. Who could give us a good idea for our sign?

Examples

NO VACATION FROM GOD
REMEMBER MY PRAYERS
JESUS, PLEASE DON'T LET ME FORGET
BLESSED MOTHER, PLEASE HELP ME
   TO REMEMBER
DEAR ANGEL, HELP ME TO PRAY

2. Devotional Practices to God
   a) First Friday

One day Jesus appeared to a very holy nun named Sister Margaret Mary. She loved our Lord with all her heart. She was sorry that everyone did not love Him too. Jesus showed Sister Margaret Mary His Sacred Heart. "Behold this Heart that has loved men so much," He said. And Jesus asked her to tell others about His Heart and about His great love for all men. So Sister Margaret Mary did tell people about the Sacred Heart of Jesus. Then Jesus told her about making the nine First Fridays. Jesus made many promises to all those who would receive Holy Communion on the First Friday of every month for nine months "in a row." Read these promises from the little book called *The Sacred Heart Promises Children All This*, by Father Lord.

We are very fortunate that we will be able to make these Nine First Fridays beginning this First Friday in June. This is one way we can show our gratitude to God for the wonderful gift of the Blessed Sacrament. Since the entire month of June is devoted to the Sacred Heart, we should receive Holy Communion often during the month to honor the Sacred Heart.

b) use of sacramentals: meaning

Hold up a Sacred Heart badge. Has anyone ever seen one of these? Do you know what it is called? Why do we wear it? This badge is called a Sacred Heart badge. It is a sacramental. A sacramental is a thing that is blessed and given to us for our use to help us to think of God, the Blessed Mother, or the saints. Your scapular that you wear is called a sacramental too. There are some things here in this room that are sacramentals. Do you think you could find them? Look for something that would help you think of Jesus, Blessed Mother, or the saints. Pictures, statues, holy water, rosaries, prayer books, blessed candles, etc., yes, all these things are called sacramentals.

This Sacred Heart badge will help us think of the Sacred Heart of Jesus whenever we look at it. We wear it to show our love for Jesus. Our scapular helps to remind us that we belong to Mary and are her children. We bless ourselves using holy water to show that we believe that Jesus died on the cross and that He will help us in all our needs.

C. Organization
1. What is prayer?
2. When should we pray?
3. What can we do that will help us to remember our prayers in the summer?
4. Who was St. Margaret Mary?
5. What should we do on the First Friday of every month?
6. What is a sacramental?
7. Name some sacramentals.

D. Virtues and Practices
1. Begin to make the nine First Fridays.
2. Say ejaculations often during the day.
3. Make use of the sacramentals.

E. Assignment
None

F. Prayer
Heart of Jesus, I put my trust in Thee! (No. 226; 300 days.)

V. SUGGESTED LEARNING ACTIVITIES
A. Tell the story of St. Margaret Mary.
B. Print signs to help children to remember their prayers during the summertime.
C. Illustrate different sacramentals.
D. Use Filmstrips: The Sacramentals.

VI. REFERENCES AND MATERIALS
A. Teacher Reference
1. *Heroines of God*, Daniel Lord, p. 18.
2. Medals, pictures of the Sacred Heart, our Blessed Mother Mary, and the saints.
3. Lord, Daniel, Rev., *The Sacred Heart Promises Children All This.*

THINGS TO KNOW

	CONTENT	PUPIL TEXT	CHURCH YEAR	PRAYERS AND HYMNS

1st DAY	A. Prayer and Devotional Practices.
	
	1. Prayers to God: review new prayers taught during the year
	2. Devotional practices:
	  a) First Friday
	  b) use of sacramentals: meaning
			Ascension Thursday	"Sacred Heart of Jesus, I put my trust in Thee."
				(No. 226; 300 days.)

2nd DAY	3. Prayers to our Blessed Mother:
	4. Devotional practices to our Blessed Mother:
	
	  a) May altar
	  b) May devotion and Crowning
	  c) First Saturday: Story of Our Lady of Fatima
	  d) use of sacramentals:
	    1) scapular and medals — *Mine* magazine (Two), May, 1953, p. 10
	    2) statues and pictures
	  e) novenas
				"Immaculate Heart of Mary, pray for us now and at the hour of our death. Amen."

3rd DAY	5. Prayers to the angels and the saints
	6. Devotional practices to the angels and the saints:
	
	  a) meaning and use of relics
	  b) use of sacramentals:
	    1) medals
	    2) statues and pictures of the angels and the saints
				"O my God, I believe in Thee, I adore Thee, I hope in Thee, and I love Thee. I ask pardon for those who do not believe, do not adore, do not hope, and who do not love Thee."
				
				(Prayer of Angel at Fatima)

4th DAY	B. Obedience to God's laws in imitation of our Blessed Mother
	
	1. Our Blessed Mother prayed: First Commandment:
	  a) how Mary honored God through prayer
	  b) things Mary prayed for:
	    1) to do God's will
	    2) to love God above all things
	    3) to love God's creatures
				"O Mary, make me to live in God, with God, and for God."
				(No. 306; 300 days.)

5th DAY				

THINGS TO DO

VIRTUES AND PRACTICES	SUGGESTED LEARNING ACTIVITIES	REFERENCES AND MATERIALS
1. Begin to make the nine First Fridays. 2. Say ejaculations to the Sacred Heart often during the day.	1. Tell the story of St. Margaret Mary. 2. Explain the picture of the Sacred Heart. 3. Promote the enthronement of the Sacred Heart in the home. 4. Suggested Filmstrip: The Sacramentals (cf. No. **67**, Unit 19).*	Morrow, *My Catholic Faith*, pp. 384–385, 366–369 (cf. No. **24**, p. 92).*
1. Make the first five Saturdays in honor of Our Lady of Fatima. 2. Faithfully wear your scapular or medal.	1. Plan and construct a May Altar with the class. 2. Have a May Crowning. 3. Write and illuminate the initial letters of — "I am the Immaculate Conception." 4. Suggested Filmstrip: Lily of Israel (cf. No. **67**, A, 928S).*	Morrow, *My Catholic Faith*, pp. 366–369 (cf. No. **24**, p. 92).* *Our Lady of Fatima* by Rev. D. Lord. Schumacher, *I Teach Catechism*, Vol. 1, p. 269 (cf. No. **10**, p. 92).*

1. Use sacramentals properly:
  a) holy water in the home
  b) blessed candles in the home
  c) crucifix in the home
  d) carry the rosary
  e) obtain blessed palm
	1. Illustrate or cut out pictures of sacramentals from religious catalogues to make booklets or a class chart.
	2. Show and discuss any relic that may be available.
		Morrow, *My Catholic Faith*, pp. 366–369 (cf. No. **24**, p. 92).*
		
		Morrow, *My Catholic Faith*, pp. 190–191 (cf. No. **24**, p. 92).*

1. Say your morning and night prayers faithfully each day.	1. Make a visit to Mary without asking her for anything, but only telling her how much you love her. 2. Make from construction paper a shrine to Blessed Mother using one of the picture studies.	Charmot, *The Presence of Mary*, pp. 84–95 (cf. No. **9**, p. 92).*

* For all keyed references in boldface type, see Teacher Bibliography, pp. 92–93, at end of this Teacher's Manual.

THINGS TO KNOW

	CONTENT	PUPIL TEXT	CHURCH YEAR	PRAYERS AND HYMNS

1st DAY	2. Our Blessed Mother loved and honored God's name: Second Commandment:
	
	a) how Mary loved the names given to Jesus, the Son of God and her Son
	b) how Mary loves the beautiful names we give to her:
	
	  1) Mother of God
	  2) Queen of the Angels and Saints
	  3) Refuge of Sinners
	  4) Comforter of the Afflicted
	  5) Our Lady of the Blessed Sacrament
	  6) Queen of Peace
				"Sweet Heart of Jesus, be my love. Sweet Heart of Mary, be my Salvation."

2nd DAY	3. Our Blessed Mother worshiped God in the Temple: Third Commandment: *a*) Mary's Presentation of the Child Jesus in the Temple *b*) Mary's Presentation in the Temple *c*) Mary's attendance at Jewish ceremonies in the Temple and in the Synagogue			"Dear Jesus, I thank You for giving me Your Blessed Mother to be my Mother too."

3rd DAY	4. Our Blessed Mother always did God's will: Fourth Commandment:
	
	a) Mary obeyed God and all those who took God's place
	b) Mary's reward for her life of perfect obedience to God's will:
	
	  1) life with Jesus: sorrows and joys:
	    (*a*) seven sorrows of Mary
	    (*b*) five joys of Mary
	  2) Mother of the Church:
	    (*a*) First Novena: Story of Pentecost
			Pentecost	Make original prayers asking our Blessed Mother to help us obey.

4th DAY	5. Our Blessed Mother is kind to everyone: Fifth Commandment: *a*) Mary showed kindness to everyone when she lived here on earth *b*) Mary shows kindness to everyone from her throne in heaven today		Trinity Sunday	Mental Prayer: 1. Picture Mary showing kindness to Jesus' little friends.
5th DAY				

THINGS TO DO

VIRTUES AND PRACTICES	SUGGESTED LEARNING ACTIVITIES	REFERENCES AND MATERIALS
1. Say a prayer to Blessed Mother whenever you see a statue or picture of her.	1. Use the time of silence while standing in line to think of Jesus and Mary. 2. Make a class chart of the titles of Blessed Mother.	Charmot, *The Presence of Mary*, pp. 28–30 (cf. No. **9**, p. 92).
1. Be faithful in assisting at Mass on all Sundays and holydays during the summer vacation.	1. Dramatize the story of "The Presentation of the Child Jesus in the Temple." 2. Read from a Bible History the story of the "Presentation" to a younger brother or sister. 3. Read and discuss the poem: The Presentation (cf. No. **60**, p. 24).	Charmot, *The Presence of Mary*, pp. 31–35 (cf. No. **9**, p. 92).
1. Obey: Right Way In Mary's Way	1. Illustrate the seven sorrows or the five joys of Mary. 2. Make a class chart or booklet of the seven sorrows or the five joys of Mary. 3. Tell the story of Pentecost.	Charmot, *The Presence of Mary*, pp. 61–93 (cf. No. **9**, p. 92).
1. Promise our Blessed Mother that you will be kind to your playmates as she was to Jesus' playmates.	1. Children draw pictures and discuss different ways in which they can be kind to their little friends. 2. Dramatize one or more of the above illustrations.	Charmot, *The Presence of Mary*, pp. 10–13, 109–111, 129–135 (cf. No. **9**, p. 92).

THINGS TO KNOW

	CONTENT	PUPIL TEXT	CHURCH YEAR	PRAYERS AND HYMNS
1st DAY	6. Our Blessed Mother is the purest of all God's creatures: Sixth and Ninth Commandments: *a)* Mary's freedom from all sin — original and actual *b)* Mary's reward for her purity		Corpus Christi	"By thy Immaculate Conception, O Mary, make my body pure and my spirit holy." (No. 358; 300 days.)

2nd DAY	7. Our Blessed Mother's love for honesty and justice: Seventh and Tenth Commandments:
	
	a) Mary showed contentment and satisfaction:
	  1) in suffering: the loss of Jesus in the temple
	  2) in poverty: the flight into Egypt
	b) Mary is generous now in obtaining graces for all men:
	  1) Mary, the Mediatrix of all graces
	  2) Mary, the Queen of the Holy Rosary
				"Virgin most powerful, pray for us."

3rd DAY	8. Our Blessed Mother is most loving and most true: Eighth Commandment:
	
	a) how Mary showed her loving thoughtfulness and consideration for others at all times: wedding feast at Cana
	b) Mary is faithful now in keeping her promises and helping those who pray to her:
	  1) all priests
	  2) her children: the faithful
			Feast of the Sacred Heart	"Mary, help of Christians, pray for us."

4th DAY	C. Faithful attendance at holy Mass. 1. Why we should be faithful 2. When we should be faithful D. Frequent reception of the sacraments of Penance and Holy Eucharist 1. When we should receive these sacraments 2. Why we should want to receive these sacraments often			"O Mary, may thy children persevere in loving thee." (No. 317; 300 days.)
5th DAY				

THINGS TO DO

VIRTUES AND PRACTICES	SUGGESTED LEARNING ACTIVITIES	REFERENCES AND MATERIALS
1. Show respect for your body by wearing modest clothing.	1. Collect pictures of boys and girls in sensible yet modest clothing; discuss how such clothing helps us to honor God who lives within us. 2. Discuss the wearing of proper (modest) clothing in the warm weather.	Charmot, *The Presence of Mary*, pp. 102–105 (cf. No. **9**, p. 92).
1. Pray for the courage to be honest at all times. 2. Be willing to share or give up personal things to make others happy.	1. Discuss the meaning of honesty and justice as taught to us by Mary. 2. Make pictures for a class chart; illustrating honesty and justice as practiced in the home and at school.	Charmot, *The Presence of Mary*, pp. 41–42 (cf. No. **9**, p. 92). Morrow, *My Catholic Faith*, pp. 382–383 (cf. No. **24**, p. 92).

1. On the first Saturday of every month pray for all priests.
2. Refuse to listen to unkind words spoken about others.
	1. Dramatize the story of the "Wedding Feast at Cana."
	2. Make a list of devotions through which we honor Mary:
	   a) Rosary
	   b) First Saturday
	   c) Novenas
	   d) Wearing of the Scapular, etc.
	3. Read and discuss the poem: The Wedding at Cana (cf. No. **60**, p. 55).
		Charmot, *The Presence of Mary*, p. 60 (cf. No. **9**, p. 92).

1. Be faithful in receiving the sacraments of Penance and Holy Eucharist during vacation time.	1. Make a "Reminder Chart" showing attendance at Sunday Mass and the reception of the sacraments during the vacation time.	Morrow, *My Catholic Faith*, pp. 202, 203, 208, 301 (cf. No. **24**, p. 92).

TEACHER BIBLIOGRAPHY

Catechism References

Elwell-Fuerst, *Jesus Comes, Our Holy Faith Series — Book Two* (Milwaukee: The Bruce Publishing Co).

Kelly-Imelda-Schumacher, *Living by God's Law* (New York: Benziger Brothers).

Heeg, Rev. Aloysius, J., S.J., *The Illustrated Catechism*, Part I (St. Louis: Catholic Mfg. Co., Inc.), 25 pp.

———— *The Illustrated Catechism*, Part II (St. Louis: Catholic Mfg. Co., Inc.), 62 pp.

———— *The Illustrated Catechism*, Part III (St. Louis: Catholic Mfg. Co., Inc.), 95 pp.

Horan, Ellamay, *A Handbook for Teachers of Religion* (New York: W. H. Sadlier, Inc., 1945), 450 pp.

Encyclical of Pope Pius X on First Communion.

Heeg, Rev. Aloysius, J., S.J., *Jesus and I*, Junior Edition (Chicago: Loyola University Press, 1934).

A Catholic Catechism, translated from the German (New York: Herder and Herder, 1957).

General Reference for the Teacher

(Keyed to Teacher's Manual — Course of Study for Grade Two)

1. Doanne, Pelagie, *A Small Child's Bible* (New York: Oxford University Press, 1946), 142 pp.
2. *The Holy Bible.*
* 3. Horan, Ellamay, *Bible Lessons* (New York: W. H. Sadlier, Inc., 1942), 250 pp.
* 4. Johnson, Rev. George, *The Bible Story* (New York: Benziger Brothers).
5. Lord, Rev. Daniel, S.J., *In the Beginning* (New York: William H. Hirten Co., Inc.), 16 pp.
6. Lord, Rev. Daniel, S.J., *Stories of the Old Testament* (New York: William H. Hirten Co., Inc.), 16 pp.
7. Louise, Sister Anna, S.S.J., *Bible Stories for Children* (Chicago: William H. Sadlier, Inc., 1941), 191 pp.
8. Raemers, Rev. S. A., *The Children's Bible History* (St. Louis: B. Herder Book Company, 1939), 193 pp.
9. Charmot, Francis, S.J., *The Presence of Mary* (South Bend: Fides Publishers, 1948), 164 pp.

Teacher Aids

10. Schumacher, Rt. Rev. Msgr., *I Teach Catechism*, Vols. 1, 2, 3 (Cincinnati: Benziger Brothers, 1946).
11. Baierl, Rev. Joseph, *The Creed Explained* (St. Paul Catechetical Press, 1943), 578 pp.
*12. Brennan, Rev. Gerald T., *Little Talks to Little Folks* (Milwaukee: The Bruce Publishing Company).

*1. *Angel Food*
2. *Angel City*
3. *Going His Way*
*4. *For Heaven's Sake*
5. *The Man Who Never Died*
6. *God Died at Three O'clock*
7. *Ghost of Kingdom Come*

13. Collins, Rev. Joseph B., Rev. Rudolph G. Bandas, *The Catechetical Instructions of St. Thomas Aquinas* (New York: Joseph F. Wagner, 1939), 200 pp.
14. Dennerle, Rev. George, *Leading Little Ones to Christ* (Milwaukee: The Bruce Publishing Company, 1932), 308 pp.
*15. Darcy, Sister Mary Jean, O.P., *Our Lady's Feasts* (New York: Sheed and Ward, 1945), 101 pp.
16. Darcy, Sister Mary Jean, O.P., *Mary, My Mother* (New York: Sheed and Ward, 1944), 165 pp.
17. Eaton, Mary, *The Little Ones* (St. Louis, Mo.: Herder Book Company).
18. Fuerst, Rt. Rev. Msgr. Anthony N., *The Systematic Teaching of Religion* (New York: Benziger Brothers, 1939), 466 pp.
19. Spirago, F., and Clarke R., *The Catechism Explained* (New York: Benziger Brothers).
20. Heeg, Aloysius J., *Practical Helps for the Religion Teacher* (St. Louis, Mo.: Queen's Work Press, 1940), 159 pp.
21. Joan, Sister Mary, O.P., *Rosary Stories for Little Folks* (Milwaukee: The Bruce Publishing Company, 1945), 32 pp.
*22. Lloyd, Teresa, *Jesus Teaching* (London: Sands and Co., 1934), 128 pp.
23. Loyola, Mother Mary, *Jesus of Nazareth* (London: Burns, Oates and Washbourne, 1906).
*24. Morrow, Rev. Louis, *My Catholic Faith* (Kenosha, Wis.: My Mission House, 1949), 407 pp.
25. O'Connor, Rev. J., S.J., *Chalk Talks* (St. Louis: Queen's Work Press).
26. Rosalia, Sister Mary, *Child Psychology and Religion* (New York: P. J. Kenedy and Sons, 1937), 138 pp.
27. Very Rev. Msgr. John D. Fitzgerald, *Jolly Jacob and other Stories* (Milwaukee: The Bruce Publishing Company, 1946), 95 pp.
28. Weiser, Rev. F. X., S.J., *Religious Customs in the Family* (Collegeville, Minn.: Liturgical Press, 1956).

Lives of Saints

29. Butler, Alban, *Lives of the Saints*, rev. ed. (New York: Kenedy and Sons, 1956), 4 volumes.

NOTE: Books indicated by an asterisk (*) should be found in every classroom.

30. Butler, Alban, *Little Pictorial Lives of the Saints* (New York: Benziger Brothers, 1930).

31. Finn, Agnes, *Stories of the Saints for Little People* (New York: Paulist Press).

32. Lord, Rev. Daniel, S.J., *Miniature Stories of the Saints* (New York: William J. Hirten Co., Inc.), Vols. I, II, III.

33. Hoever, Rev. Hugo S., S.O.C., *Lives of the Saints* (New York: Catholic Book Publishing Co., 1955).

34. Lord, Rev. Daniel, S.J., *Heroes and Heroines of God's Church* (New York: Wm. J. Hirten Co., Inc., 1946).

35. Patrice, Sister Margaret, *Up the Shining Path* (Milwaukee: The Bruce Publishing Company, 1946), 173 pp.

36. Steedman, Amy, *In God's Garden* (New York: Thomas Nelson and Sons), 142 pp.

37. Treacy, Rev. Gerald G., *Stories of Great Saints for Children* (New York: The Paulist Press, pamphlet), 32 pp.

38. Vera, Mother Mary, S.N.D., *First Grade Course of Study in Religion*.

39. Windeatt, Mary Fabyan, *Children of Fatima* (Paterson, N. J.: St. Anthony Press).

40. Windeatt, Mary Fabyan, *Little Queen* (Indianapolis: St. Meinrad Abbey).

41. Windeatt, Mary Fabyan, *Little Sister* (Indianapolis: St. Meinrad Abbey, 1944), 81 pp.

42. Windham, Joan, *Saints Who Spoke English* (New York: Sheed and Ward, 1939), 134 pp.

First Communion Stories

43. Collins, Rev. Joseph, B., S.S., *Jesus Loves Children* (Milwaukee: The Bruce Publishing Company, 1942), 128 pp.

44. Cook, Frederick, *The Rosary for Little Fingers* (New Jersey: St. Anthony Guild Press, 1944), 37 pp.

*45. Dooley, Rev. L. M., S.V.D., *Hello Halo* (Duxbury, Mass.: Lumen Press).

46. Herbst, Rev. Winfrid, *Christ's Little Ones* (St. Nazianz, Wis.: The Salvatorian Fathers, 1937), 231 pp.

47. Kelly, Rev. William R., *Our Sacraments* (New York: Benziger Brothers).

*48. LeBuffe, Rev. Francis P., *Let's Try Mental Prayer* (St. Louis, Mo.: The Queen's Work), 37 pp.

49. Loyola, Mother Mary, *First Communion and After* (New York: Benziger Brothers).

50. Sister M. Adrine Welters, O.S.B., *Pax* (Milwaukee: The Bruce Publishing Company, 1952).

51. Drinkwater, F. H., Rev., *Catechism Stories* (Westminster, Md.: Newman Press, 1948), 480 pp.

52. McDonald, Mary Reynold, *Little Stories About God* (St. Paul, Minn.: Catechetical Guild), 64 pp.

*53. Morrow, Most Rev. Louis, *Our First Communion* (New York: Ed. O'Toole Company).

*54. Notre Dame Sisters, *First Communion Days* (St. Louis, Mo.: Herder Book Company).

55. Notre Dame Sisters, *The Eager Hearts* (St. Louis, Mo.: Herder Book Company).

56. Notre Dame Sisters, *True Stories for First Communicants* (St. Louis, Mo.: Herder Book Company).

Poems

*57. Belger, Sister Mary Josita, O.S.F., *Sing a Song of Holy Things* (Milwaukee: The Tower Press, 5701 W. Washington Blvd., 1945), 111 pp.

58. Fitzpatrick, E. A., *Religious Poems for Little Folks* (Milwaukee: The Bruce Publishing Company).

59. Lord, Rev. Daniel, *Chants for Children* (St. Louis, Mo.: Queen's Work Press).

60. Moran, B. J., *Verses for Tiny Tots* (Milwaukee: The Bruce Publishing Company, 1937).

61. Patrice, Sister Margaret, S.S.J., *A Lovely Gate Set Wide* (Milwaukee: The Bruce Publishing Company).

*62. Thayer, Mary Dixon, *A Child on His Knees* (New York: Macmillan Company, 1948).

63. World Library of Sacred Music, *People's Hymnal*, Cincinnati 14, Ohio.

64. McLaughlin and Reilly, *Pius X Hymnal*, Boston, Mass.

65. Richter, Ada, *My First Hymnal* (Boston, Mass.: McLaughlin and Reilly, 45 Franklin St.).

Audio-Visual Aids

66. Religious Song Guild, "Commandments and Sacraments" (record), Paterson, N. J., 1956.

67. Society for Visual Education, Inc., Chicago 14, Ill., Catholic catalogue.

68. R. C. A. Victor Youth Series, Camden, N. J.

69. Catholic Children's Record Club, The Story of Jesus Christ, Disk of the Month Club, Inc., Tuckahoe, N. Y.

70. Brian Press, Inc., St. John's Catechism Filmstrip Series, Garden City, N. Y.

71. New Catholic Filmstrip, Eye Gate House Inc., Jamaica 35, N. Y.

72. Catechetical Guild, St. Paul, Minn.

73. St. Anthony Guild, Paterson, N. J., *Life of Christ*.

74. Our Lady of Grace Society, Religious Picture Service, Gouppy, Lowell, Mass.

75. Thomas Nelson and Sons, *188 Pictures from the Old and New Testament*, 381 4th Avenue, New York.

GENERAL REFERENCES FOR CHILDREN

First Books for Little Catholics (Series), Catechetical Guild Educational Society, St. Paul 1, Minn.

1. My Little Missal
2. Let's Pray
3. A First Life of Christ
4. The Rosary
5. My Confession
6. God's Story Book
7. Hail Mary
8. I Believe
9. A First Book of Saints
10. Listen to God

Bedier, J., *My Book About God* (New York: Macmillan Company).

Doanne, Pelagie, *A Small Child's Bible* (New York: Oxford University Press, 1946), 142 pp.

Doyle, Rev. C. H., *Do You Know Jesus?* (Paterson, N. J.: St. Anthony Guild Press).

Ellard, G., S.J., and Heeg, A., S.J., *The Story of the Mass* (New York: Devotional Publishing Company).

Francis, Father, *The King Comes*, Milwaukee 15, Wisconsin, 32 pp.

Henry, Sister, O.S.D., *Book I* (*Rosary Readers*) (Chicago: Ginn and Company).

Hornback, Florence M., *When We Say the Hail Mary* (Paterson, N. J.: St. Anthony Guild Press).

——— *When We Say the Our Father* (Paterson, N. J.: St. Anthony Guild Press).

Lord, Rev. Daniel A., *A Catholic Child Believes* (New York: Devotional Publishing Company, 1952).

——— *I'd Like You to Meet My Family* (New York: William J. Hirten Co., Inc.), 8 pp.

——— *In the Beginning* (New York: William J. Hirten Co., Inc.), 16 pp.

——— *Jesus, the Hero* (New York: William J. Hirten Co., Inc., 1943), 24 pp.

——— *Miniature Lives of the Saints*, 4 vols. (New York: William J. Hirten Co., Inc.).

——— *Stories from the Old Testament* (New York: William J. Hirten Co., Inc.), 16 pp.

——— *Story of Christmas* (New York: William J. Hirten Co., Inc.), 6 pp.

——— *The Great Deeds of Jesus* (New York: William J. Hirten Co., Inc., 1943), 22 pp.

——— *The Stories of the Angels* (New York: William J. Hirten Co., Inc.), 6 pp.

——— *The Story of the Blessed Virgin* (New York: William J. Hirten Co., Inc., 1944), 6 pp.

——— *The Story of the Holy Family* (New York: William J. Hirten Co., Inc., 1944), 6 pp.

——— *The Story of the Sacred Heart* (New York: William J. Hirten Co., Inc.), 6 pp.

——— *The Story of St. Joseph* (New York: William J. Hirten Co., Inc., 1944), 6 pp.

——— *When Our Lord Was a Boy* (New York: William J. Hirten Co., Inc.) (new Catholic Bible Series).

McDonald, Mary Reynolds, *Little Stories About God* (St. Paul, Minn.: Catechetical Guild), 64 pp.

Michel, Dom Virgil, Dom Basil Stegmann, Sisters of the Order of St. Dominic, *Jesus, Our Savior* (New York: Macmillan Co., 1934).

Morrow, Most Rev. Louis, *My First Communion* (New York: Ed O'Toole Company).

Notre Dame School Sisters, *Children — Their Helpers* (Chicago: Heath and Company).

——— *Life of My Savior* (Milwaukee: The Bruce Publishing Company).

——— *Life of My Savior* (Highway for Heaven Series) (Milwaukee: The Bruce Publishing Company).

Sisters of St. Dominic, *Jesus Our Savior* (Christ Life Series) (Macmillan, 1942).

Wagenhauser, Nita, *Little Stories of Christ's Passion* (New Jersey: St. Anthony Guild Press, 1941), 112 pp.

——— *Miracles* (New Jersey: St. Anthony Guild Press), 112 pp.

CPSIA information can be obtained
at www.ICGtesting.com
Printed in the USA
BVHW060018100519
547827BV00010B/284/P